GW00599035

Cuba

Cuba

Text by Fred Mawer
Revised by Neil Schlecht
Photography: Neil Schlecht pages 3, 4, 5, 9, 10,
23, 24, 27, 28, 34, 36, 38, 39, 40, 43,
45, 46, 56, 58, 61, 62, 66, 70, 73, 76,
83, 89; Fred Mawer pages 6, 13, 16,
20, 31, 32, 49, 51, 53, 55, 65, 69, 78,
86, 93, 94, 97, 100
Layout: Media Content Marketing, Inc.
Cartography by Raffaele De Gennaro
Managing Editor: Tony Halliday

Nintth Edition 2003 (reprinted)

CONTACTING THE EDITORS
Every effort has been made to provide accurate information in this publication, but changes are inevitable. The publisher cannot be responsible for any resulting loss, inconvenience or injury. We would appreciate it if readers would call our attention to any errors or outdated information by contacting Apa Publications, PO Box 7910, London SE1 1WE, England. Fax: (44) 20 7403 0290;

© 2003 Apa Publications GmbH & Co. Verlag KG, Singapore Branch, Singapore

Printed in Singapore by Insight Print Services (Pte) Ltd, 38 Joo Koon Road, Singapore 628990. Tel: (65) 6865-1600. Fax: (65) 6861-6438

Berlitz Trademark Reg. U.S. Patent Office and other countries. Marca Registrada. Used under licence from the Berlitz Investment Corporation

CONTENTS

● A (☞) in the text denotes a highly recommended sight

Cuba

CUBA AND ITS PEOPLE

The largest island in the Caribbean, Cuba is blessed with palm trees, sultry temperatures, hip-swiveling rhythms, pristine beaches, a surfeit of rum, and the world's finest hand-rolled cigars. But it's nearly impossible to think of Cuba only in those hedonistic terms—even if you're merely headed to one of the island's tourist resorts.

For much of the 20th century, Cuba occupied a leading role on the world stage wholly disproportionate to its small size and lack of economic clout. From the overthrow of the dictator Fulgencio Batista in 1959 to Fidel Castro's tenacious hold on power and declarations of socialism, this small Caribbean nation has assumed near-mythical status as a living laboratory of social experimentation, political defiance, and a people's perseverance.

For half a century a combative Castro has weathered the opposition of the US government and the hostility of Cuban exiles in Miami, just 90 miles to the north. The Cuban people have been required to make repeated sacrifices in the face of the ongoing American trade embargo and the collapse of the Soviet Union's support and trade. Cuba is still standing, even though many of its crumbling colonial edifices remain just barely upright.

As one of the last Communist hold-outs in the world, this complex nation of 11 million is an enduring curiosity. With much of the rest of the planet racing ahead at a dizzying digital pace, Cuba crawls along in a slow-motion time warp. Behemoth vintage American automobiles from the 1940s and 1950s, patched and propped up, lumber down the streets of dimly lit cities. In rural areas cars give way to oxen-led carts, wobbly iron bicycles, and pedicabs. Houses are equipped with the most rudimentary, ancient appliances imaginable. Septets of octogenarian musicians play wonderfully addictive Cuban *son,* rhythms unchanged since the 1930s.

Cuba is inseparable from the politics of the latter half of the 20th century. Children are sworn in at the age of six to become Young Communist Pioneers. Throughout the country giant billboards function like pep talks from the government, proclaiming "*Socialismo o Muerte*" ("Socialism or Death") and "*Viva la Revolución*" ("Long Live the Revolution"). Portraits of Che Guevara, the 1960s revolutionary martyr, and Fidel Castro, the longest-surviving head of state in the world, are plastered on the walls of shops, offices, and homes.

Everything has always creaked and sputtered in hard-pressed Communist Cuba. But now that it's no longer propped up by a sympathetic Soviet Union, the cracks are really showing. Government rations don't suffice. Many families live in appallingly overcrowded conditions, and couples seeking privacy rent out rooms in *posadas,* or "love hotels," by the hour. Most people earn no more than $15 a month, paid in the increasingly worthless Cuban currency, the peso. Nearly every doorstoop is crowded with idle workers, either unable to put their state educations to good use or preferring to scramble for occasional (often extralegal) odd jobs.

Forty years after the revolution, Cubans still form long queues for bread and are limited to what their measly ration booklets permit: six pounds of rice and sugar, 20 ounces of beans, two

Currency Matters

Visitors need US dollars in Cuba as anything connected with tourism (hotels, souvenirs, museums, etc) is charged in dollars. However, it's a good idea to have a supply of Cuban pesos for shopping from street vendors or at markets. The terms can be confusing: "pesos" usually refer not to pesos but to US dollars. A dollar (dólar) is also called "divisa." To clarify, the Cuban peso—the national currency—is called "peso cubano."

bottles of cooking oil, some bread, plus some cigarettes, coffee, and a few other goods. Everything else—a bit of pork, some chicken, decent shoes—must be purchased on the black market or in dollar-only stores.

Until 1993 it was illegal for Cubans to hold US currency. Since then, much of the economy has been given over to the almighty dollar, with many products and foodstuffs available only in dollar stores. (It is obvious which ones are the dollar stores: they are considerably nicer and better lighted than peso stores, with a much

Today's Cuban cities make it easy to believe that you have traveled back in time.

greater selection of Western goods.) The need for dollars has created a new "us vs. them" rift in society, and there is now a deepening divide separating the have-nots from those Cubans with access to dollars, either through family members who send remittances from abroad or who have jobs in foreign businesses or tourism that provide tips or wages in US currency.

The glaring deficiencies of the Cuban economy and needs of the Cuban people are impossible to ignore. Still, one doesn't see the blinding, heart-wrenching poverty in Cuba common in places like Bangladesh, India, and even other parts of Latin America. Housing is provided by the state—you are unlikely to see homeless people sleeping on the streets anywhere in Cuba—and while Cubans don't get nearly enough with their ration books, they have something to eat, and many appear surprisingly well dressed. No doubt the few dollars earned on the side or sent by family members help ease the pain.

Cuba is not without its successes. The 1959 revolution envisioned sweeping social changes, and several of its achievements would be worthy of praise in First World countries, let alone undeveloped nations. All Cubans are entitled to free health care. Education is free and available to all, and Cuba's university system has produced some of the world's finest medical and science professionals. Average life expectancy rose from 57 years in 1958 to 75 in 1992—the highest in Latin America—while the number of people per doctor decreased from 5,000 in 1958 to 400 in 1988. Infant mortality (7.89 per 1,000 births) is the lowest in Latin America and the equal of many developed countries. Literacy rates improved from 76

Although tourists need not wait in line for government rations, it is routine for the Cuban people.

percent of the population in 1958 to 95 percent in 1992. Violent crime is enviably low.

However, Cubans enjoy no real freedom of speech, freedom of the press, or freedom to travel outside the country, as opponents of the socialist regime outside of Cuba—and growing numbers of people in Cuba—are only too happy to tell you. There's a single political party. Every year hundreds attempt risky flight to the US mainland in rickety *balseros* (rafts), and thousands more line up at the US Interests Office in Havana and at other foreign embassies in a desperate lottery for exit visas.

In dire need of hard currency, Cuba has embraced tourism. Compared with less than a quarter of a million visitors in 1985, some two million tourists arrived in 2000. Tourism has surpassed the sugar industry to become the country's top revenue earner. Yet large-scale tourism is still nascent in Cuba. Most travelers still opt for package tours and remain ensconced in tourist enclaves clustered on beaches.

Cuba's dilapidation, poverty, and restrictions only serve to highlight the indomitable spirit of the Cuban people. They are blessed with a remarkable resiliency, forbearance, and joy that no economic hardship seems capable of dimming. Cubans are as hospitable a people as you'll find, inviting visitors into their cramped homes given half a chance. Everywhere there are bubbly school children—outfitted in identical maroon or mustard-colored uniforms—racing around the streets, playing pick-up games of stickball, or amusing themselves with improvised skateboards and kites.

Whether or not its people are prepared for it, at the beginning of the 21st century Cuba has finally arrived at the twilight of the Castro era. It's anybody's guess what will happen when this stalwart of the *Revolución* finally relinquishes power. Most believe that Cuba will be forced to emerge from its cocoon. But for the time being, Cuba remains an adventure as well as an anachronism.

A BRIEF HISTORY

W hen Christopher Columbus disembarked on eastern Cuba on 27 October 1492, he quickly penned a note exclaiming that the land was "the most lovely that eyes have ever seen." Indian tribes including the Siboney from Central and South America had lived on the island since at least 1000 B.C.

In 1511 Diego de Velázquez sailed from neighboring Hispaniola with some 300 *conquistadores* (conquerors). Baracoa became the first of seven settlements across Cuba. Velázquez and his followers enslaved the native peoples and in the process exposed them to European diseases. Whole villages committed suicide, and by the mid-1500s the Indian population had declined from over 100,000 to 3,000.

Piracy and Trade

Until the end of the 16th century, Cuba remained a fairly insignificant Spanish colony. The port cities Havana and Santiago de Cuba were heavily fortified to defend against French and English pirate raids. Considerable contraband trade originated from bases around the island.

In 1762 British forces captured Havana. They held it for only a year before returning it to Spain in exchange for Florida, but during this period trade was opened up to additional markets, notably the North American colonies. A lucrative tobacco industry had taken hold in Cuba, and after 1763 the sugar-cane business skyrocketed. Though settlers brought the first African slaves to Cuba in the early 1500s, hundreds of thousands of African laborers were imported in the late 18th century to meet the demands of the sugar industry.

By the middle of the 19th century, Cuba produced a third of the world's sugar and was considered one of the most valuable colonies in the world. Half a million slaves—nearly

The colonial atmosphere at Morro Castle in Santiago has been maintained since the 16th century.

half the population—worked the plantations, and at least 3,500 trading ships visited Cuba annually.

The Road to Independence

Spaniards born and raised in Cuba, known as *criollos* (creoles), managed the sugar-cane plantations but were not involved in the running of the country. During the 19th century some criollos (particularly in Oriente, the island's poorer, eastern region) became increasingly disenchanted and desired greater autonomy.

On 10 October 1868 Carlos Manuel de Céspedes, a criollo plantation owner who had already had a brief role in uprisings in Spain, issued a call for independence and liberated slaves from his estate, La Demajagua. During the subsequent Ten Years' War (1868–78) 50,000 Cubans—including Céspedes—and more than 200,000 Spanish lost their lives. Cuba remained a colony of Spain, but the war contributed to the abolition of slavery on the island in 1886 and planted the seeds of a national consciousness.

In 1895 José Martí, Cuba's most venerated patriot (who now has a street, square, or building named after him in every town), led the next and most important uprising against Spain. Born in 1853 and exiled at 18 for his political views, Martí became a journalist and poet. From exile in the United States he argued for Cuban independence. Martí was killed in an ambush during the War of Independence, which began in 1895 and in which some 300,000 Cubans died.

Throughout the 19th century, the United States, keenly interested in the island's strategic significance and its sugar market, had become increasingly involved in Cuban affairs. A US purchase of the island from Spain had long been on the agenda, even though Martí had warned of becoming a satellite of the United States ("I know the Monster, because I have lived in its lair," he wrote).

In February 1898 the *U.S.S. Maine* was sunk in Havana's harbor, killing all 260 crew members. Although Spanish responsibility was never incontrovertibly established, the United States used the sinking as a pretext to declare war. US victory came swiftly, with Spain surrendering claim to the island by the end of the same year. A provisional military government lasted to 1902, when Cuba became an independent republic.

False Independence

For the next five decades the United States, the largest importer of Cuban sugar, dominated the island's economy and largely controlled its political processes. The period was rife with political corruption, violence, and terrorism. After 1933 Fulgencio Batista, though only a sergeant, orchestrated the strings of power through a series of puppet presidents before winning the presidency outright in 1940. He retired in 1944 but returned by staging a military coup in 1952. His venal dictatorship made it possible for him to invest some $300 million abroad by 1959.

Che and Fidel: Brothers in Revolution

Ernesto "Che" Guevara (*che* meaning "mate" or "buddy" in Argentine slang) is the official poster boy and martyr of the Cuban revolution, idolized by Cubans. His dramatic, beret-topped visage is seen on billboards and photographs throughout Cuba. Born in 1928 in Argentina, Guevara trained as a doctor before embarking on nomadic treks through South and Central America with a pile of Marxist literature in his rucksack. He met Castro in Mexico in 1955 and for the next 10 years was Castro's right-hand man, as a guerrilla in the mountains then as director of the national bank (signing bills as, simply, "Che"), minister of industry, and minister of the economy. In 1965, he abandoned Cuba for new causes. He was killed trying to foment revolt in Bolivia in 1967.

Fidel Castro—president of Cuba, secretary-general of its Communist Party, and commander-in-chief of its armed forces—was born in 1927 and trained as a lawyer at the University of Havana. The world's youngest leader in 1959, Castro has defied all expectations to become the longest-serving head of state on the planet. Fidel, as he is known to all, is a towering but frustrating patriarchal figure to Cubans. Yet he remains, above all, *El Comandante*.

A few years ago Fidel finally gave up his beloved cigars, saying they were great for the Cuban economy "but not so great for my health." Now in his mid-70s, this former guerrilla fighter and consummate firebrand can still speak articulately without notes from a platform for hours. Fidel has outlasted eight American presidents despite a fabled list of CIA assassination attempts—including one involving exploding cigars.

Since the 1920s disillusionment with the nascent republic —with its clear dependence on the United States and its lack of political probity or social equality—had grown steadily. Although Cuba had the second-highest per capita income in Latin America, prosperity did not filter down from the upper classes. In fact, the World Bank in 1950 declared as many as 60 percent of Cubans undernourished. In Havana there was a greater concentration of millionaires than anywhere else in Central or South America, and the capital was dubbed "an offshore Las Vegas" for its brothels, casinos, and gangsters.

The Road to Revolution

On 26 July 1953, rebels attacked the Moncada Barracks (the country's second most important military base) in Santiago de Cuba. The assault was a failure, but it thrust into the limelight its young leader, Fidel Castro. Castro was imprisoned and put on trial; his legendary two-hour defense speech, later published as *History Will Absolve Me,* became a revolutionary manifesto. Castro was incarcerated on the Isle of Pines (now called the Isla de la Juventud) until May 1955, when Batista granted an amnesty to political prisoners.

Castro then fled to Mexico. The following year he returned to southeastern Cuba with a force of 81 guerrillas (including Che Guevara) crammed onto a small yacht, the *Granma.* Only 15 reached

Cubans are on a first-name basis with President Castro, known to all as "Fidel."

the Sierra Maestra mountains safely. Incredibly, from such inauspicious beginnings the so-called "26 of July Movement" grew into a serious guerrilla army, aided in no small part by local peasants who were promised land reform.

Following a disastrous offensive by government troops on the rebels' mountain strongholds in 1958, on 1 January 1959 Batista fled the country for the Dominican Republic. The *barbudos* (the bearded ones) triumphantly entered Santiago, then marched into Havana one week later.

Castro's Cuba

Castro's fledgling government immediately ordered rents reduced, new wage levels set, and estates limited in size to 390 hectares (966 acres). A comprehensive nationalization program followed, and the government expropriated factories, utilities, and more land. The foundations were set for near-universal state employment. At the same time, the new government instituted sweeping, enlightened programs to eradicate illiteracy and provide free universal schooling and health care.

A centralized, all-powerful state didn't please all Cubans. The media were soon placed under state control, promised elections were never held, and Committees for the Defense of the Revolution (CDRs) were established to keep tabs on dissenters. In the early years of the revolution, tens of thousands of people suspected of being unsympathetic to its goals were detained, imprisoned, or sent to labor camps, along with such other "undesirables" as homosexuals and priests.

Between 1959 and 1962 approximately 200,000 Cubans, primarily professionals and affluent landowners, fled the country. Expatriate Cubans settled in nearby Florida, establishing a colony that would steadily gain in political and economic power. Another 200,000 abandoned Cuba as part of the Freedom Flights Program between 1965 and 1971, and

125,000—a good number of whom were said to be criminals—followed in 1980, when Castro lifted travel restrictions from the port of Mariel (west of Havana).

According to official Washington estimates, US businesses lost $8 billion as a result of Cuba's state appropriations and seizing of assets. In retaliation, the US government launched a trade embargo in 1960 against Cuba that continues to this day. In 1961 CIA-trained Cuban exiles attempted an overthrow of Castro's regime, resulting in the Bay of Pigs fiasco.

Washington remained fundamentally opposed to Cuba's political evolution and sought to isolate Castro in Latin America. Soon after the Bay of Pigs, Castro declared himself a Marxist-Leninist. Castro had not displayed any Communist inclinations in the 1950s, and some suggest that US aggression pushed him to ingratiate himself with the powerful Soviet Union and its Eastern block of potential trading partners. By the end of the 1980s, more than 80 percent of Cuban trade was with the USSR, which also provided Cuba with a subsidy of state support worth an estimated US$5 billion annually.

In 1962 Soviet president Nikita Khrushchev installed 42 medium-range nuclear missiles in Cuba. US president John F. Kennedy imposed a naval blockade on the island to ensure no more missiles arrived and insisted that the existing ones be removed. After six days of eyeball-to-eyeball challenge (now known in the US as the "Cuban Missile Crisis"), the potential nuclear disaster was averted when Khrushchev backed down in return for a US promise never to invade Cuba.

The Special Period

Until the end of the 1980s, Soviet trade and subsidies were crucial factors in propping up Cuba's heavily centralized and often badly planned economy. But the subsequent dismantling of the Soviet Union suddenly left Cuba bereft of food, oil, and hard currency.

The Cuban government announced the start of a peacetime "Special Period" in 1990, introducing new austerity measures. Though rationing had existed since the early 1960s, it was increased to cover many more basic items. It became virtually impossible for Cubans to live on rations alone. To make matters worse, in 1992 the Cuba Democracy Act extended the US embargo to cover a ban on trade with Cuba for foreign subsidiaries of US companies.

With its economy in disarray, the government introduced a limited number of capitalist measures while maintaining a firm political grip. Foreign investment, in the form of joint ventures in the fields of tourism and mineral and oil exploration, was keenly encouraged.

The dangers of exposure to foreign opinion and "moral corruption" from the rapidly expanding tourism industry is now viewed as a necessary evil. The adoption of measures such as the legalization of the dollar and small-scale private

The Bay of Pigs Invasion

On 17 April 1961, a force of 1,297 Cuban exiles landed at Playa Girón. The Cubans were CIA-trained and came from US. ships waiting offshore; US-piloted planes had bombed Cuban airfields days before. President Kennedy was unwilling to commit US troops on the ground or order further air strikes (US participation was denied at every stage). Castro's 20,000 troops, assisted by artillery and tanks, repelled the invasion within just 48 hours. Some 1,180 exiles were captured and ransomed for US$53 million worth of food and medicine. The victory greatly boosted Castro's domestic and international status. Soon after, he declared Cuba a socialist, one-party state.

enterprises in 1993, and the introduction of private farmers' markets in 1994, have improved the welfare of some Cubans. The situation for others, with no access to dollars, has turned increasingly desperate.

No doubt many Cubans would emigrate if allowed to do so. In August 1994 Castro suddenly lifted restrictions on those wishing to leave (coastal patrols usually force potential émigrés to return). More than 30,000 Cubans tried to cross shark-infested waters to Florida on improvised rafts. Facing a dramatic influx of Cubans, President Clinton abolished the US policy of automatic asylum to Cuban refugees, placing them in a makeshift tent settlement in Guantánamo Bay Naval Base.

In the opinion of many, Cuba is an isolated socialist dinosaur. Yet it—and its aging leader—soldier on against all odds. The US embargo, denounced by an ever-increasing majority in the United Nations, is spurred on by vehement anti-Castro lobbying by Cubans in southern Florida. Still, changes in the status quo seem likely. But nearly four decades after the Cuban missile crisis, the world continues to wait, wondering whether a lifting of US trade and tourism sanctions or a change in leadership in Cuba will arrive first.

The Guantánamo Bay Naval Base is under high security at all times.

Historical Landmarks

1492 Christopher Columbus lands in eastern Cuba.

1511 Diego Velázquez begins Spanish settlement.

1519 Founding of Havana on its present site.

1868–78 Ten Years' War for Cuban independence, ends with Spanish victory.

1886 End of slavery in Cuba.

1895 War of Independence begins; José Martí killed.

1898 Sinking of the *U.S.S. Maine*; US defeats Spain, which surrenders Cuba.

1902 Formation of the Republic of Cuba.

1940–44 Fulgencio Batista rules as president dictator.

1953 Fidel Castro launches failed attack on the Moncada Barracks (26 July).

1959 Castro seizes power (1 January); Batista flees.

1961 CIA-trained Cuban exiles defeated at the Bay of Pigs.

1962 Cuban Missile Crisis.

1990 Soviet trade and subsidies disappear; new austerity measures of Special Period begin.

1993 Economic reforms begin, including acceptance of US dollars as currency in Cuba.

1994 Exodus of 30,000 rafters to Florida; most are re turned to Guantánamo Bay Naval Base.

1995 More reforms: farmers are allowed to sell food di rectly to consumers, and real estate may be sold to foreigners.

1996 US passes Helms-Burton law forbidding US companies from doing business with Cuba.

1998 Pope John Paul II visits Cuba.

2002 Ex-US President Jimmy Carter visits Cuba.

WHERE TO GO

To the surprise of many first-time visitors, Cuba is no speck in the Caribbean. Nicolás Guillén, the nation's finest poet, described the island as a "long green alligator." Long it certainly is, at 1,250 km (776 miles) from snout to tail. Nearly the size of England, Cuba is divided into 14 provinces and incorporates some 1,500 offshore islands, known as *cayos* ("cays" or "keys").

Given its size, you would need at least a month to explore Cuba fully. Most people begin their journeys in the capital, Havana, before heading to the prized tobacco lands farther west and doubling back across the plains of sugar cane and some of the country's finest colonial towns in central Cuba. The eastern region, known as Oriente, has soaring mountains and Cuba's second and most musical city, Santiago de Cuba.

Resort hotels hug quintessential Caribbean beaches around the whole island, and though many package tourists still stick close to the coasts, every region has charming, engaging towns. Sand and sun Cuba certainly has, but most visitors who dare to step away from the beach will find it simply too beguiling to spend a whole holiday lying idly in front of their hotels.

HAVANA (LA HABANA)

The island's capital, with almost 3 million inhabitants, is one of the most intoxicating cities in the world. Ever since its early maritime days and through the 1950s—when gangsters who ran prostitution and gambling rackets made Havana synonymous with decadence—it has always held a slightly seedy, languorous allure. That nostalgic appeal is still evident.

Today Havana is a one-of-a-kind, fascinating study in decay. Unrestrained ocean waves and salty sea spray have wrecked

A fresh coat of paint on the colonial buildings of Old Havana enhances the neighborhood's quaint feel.

huge chunks of the Malecón, the sumptuous promenade and roadway that traces the edge of the sea. Throughout the city, crumbling houses three and four stories tall, somehow still standing, line backstreets where children play stickball and their parents and grandparents hover around doorstoops. In Old Havana, magnificently restored colonial palaces and stately baroque churches and convents crowd pulsating squares. Once the finest colonial city in the Americas, Havana's grandeur has not been destroyed even by decades of crisis and neglect. No less defiant than Castro himself, beneath the rubble this city is a living, breathing, vital, and sensual creature.

Havana sprawls over more than 700 square km (270 square miles) and is divided into five districts. Those of greatest interest are Habana Vieja (Old Havana), Centro Habana (Central

Havana), Vedado, and—to a lesser extent—Miramar. The latter two districts are newer residential and shopping barrios that extend west and south of the old city. While most areas within a neighborhood can be covered comfortably on foot, passing from one to the other usually requires a taxi or *bicitaxi;* the latter is Cuba's bicycle taxi, a type of pedicab.

Old Havana (La Habana Vieja)

The oldest section of Havana is the city's most spectacular, even if restoration work and gleaming coats of pastel colonial colors (plus a stern police presence on every corner) are leaving parts of it with a slightly more sanitized feel than the weathered working class neighborhoods that extend along the water and inland. As the location of the city's greatest

The Plaza de la Catedral (Cathedral Square) bustles with activity at the foot of the towering Baroque façade.

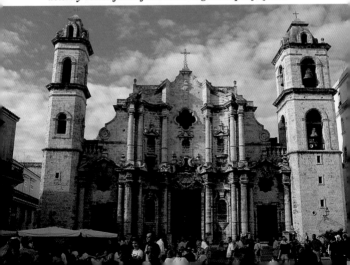

historical sites, **Old Havana** is where you'll want to spend most of your time if it is limited.

Havana was founded along a vast natural harbor in 1519. During the 16th century a fleet of galleons laden with treasures used the port as a pit stop on the way back to Spain from the New World. By the 17th century pirate attacks prompted the building of extensive city defenses—colossal forts, a chain across the harbor mouth, and prominent city walls—making Havana the "Bulwark of the West Indies."

The wealthiest residents lived with their slaves in grand mansions constructed in *mudéjar* style, a Christian-Muslim architectural tradition dating from medieval Spain. Hidden courtyards bathed in penumbral light lurked behind massive doors, slatted blinds, carved iron window bars *(rejas),* and half-moon stained-glass windows *(mediopuntos).*

The presence of such architectural wonders, no matter how dilapidated, led UNESCO to declare Old Havana a World Heritage Site in 1982. In the central tourist quarter, an expanding number of buildings are being spruced up with the assistance of UNESCO and foreign foundations, but many others are propped up by wooden columns, lean-tos that appear to be merely forestalling the inevitable. Their arcades, fluted pillars, and mosaic tiles are teetering on last legs, praying for restoration miracles. At night the deep darkness of the streets is punctuated only by the neon glow of TV sets from tiny front rooms and the occasional headlights of a small colony of gas-guzzling vintage Chevrolets and Plymouths.

Havana's distant era lives on. Legendary places plucked from the pages of popular novels and the lives of fiction writers need little input from visitors to evoke their storied past: Graham Greene's **Hotel Sevilla,** where "Our Man in Havana" went to meet his secret service contact, and Hemingway's favorite watering holes (El Floridita and La Bodeguita del Medio) and the **Hotel Ambos Mundos,** where he penned much of *For Whom the Bell Tolls.*

Old Havana is best experienced on foot, although you can also pick up a *bicitaxi* (pedicab) to get to the Malecón or the museums at the district's edge.

Plaza de la Catedral

Havana's delicious **Cathedral Square,** the focus of Habana Vieja life, could be a stage set. Most days a colorful crafts mar-

---

Santería: The Cult of the Gods

Santería ("saint worship") is a syncretic religion derived from the Yoruba people in Nigeria and developed in Cuba by African slaves. Practitioners worship a complex pantheon of deities (*orishás*), each with a specific character and a parallel Catholic saint—a guise that allowed slaves to disguise the religion from their hostile owners.

Worshippers affiliate themselves to a particular *orishá*, wearing colored necklaces and maintaining shrines in their homes. The saints are believed to exercise control over virtually every aspect of a person's life, but to communicate with them, believers need the assistance of a *santero* (priest), who will throw shells and perform other rituals to learn of the saints' commands. Saints' days are celebrations featuring Afro-Cuban drum beating and dancing.

Perhaps as many as 90 percent of Cubans have at one time practiced the rituals of santería—including, it is alleged, even Castro. While difficult to quantify, its popularity appears to be on the increase: the number of practitioners is thought to rival or even surpass that of Roman Catholics. In many parts of Cuba, one can see people wearing the colored beads of their saint—red and white for Changó, the powerful god of war, and blue and white for Yemayá, the goddess of the sea—and others dressed all in white for initiation rights "to become sainted."

---

ket spreads across the cobbled square, and tourists linger at El Patio's outdoor café, sipping *mojitos* and tapping their toes to a sampling of Cuban *son*. The all-hours hubbub here is infectious. The glorious baroque façade and asymmetrical belltowers of the late 18th-century cathedral are only marginally the square's top attraction. Yet the church, begun by Jesuits in 1748, is a thing of beauty; one half expects its bells to erupt in triumphant song. Its clean interior is surprisingly plain, but it once held the remains of Christopher Columbus. Just south of the cathedral are superb colonial mansions with bright

Folkloric dancers show off their colorful garb in Havana's oldest square.

shutters and *mediopuntos,* and an attractive little cul-de-sac (**Callejón de Chorro**) with a graphic arts workshop.

Of particular interest in the Cathedral Square is the **Museo de Arte Colonial,** housed in a handsome palace dating to 1720. Its yellow courtyard and little-altered architectural features are complemented by a large collection of 17th- and 18th-century furniture.

Just round the corner, on Calle Empedrado (at no. 207), you'll find the atmospheric bar-restaurant **La Bodeguita del Medio** (see page 41), which according to Hemingway served Havana's finest *mojito* (management apparently believes the notoriety is worth an extra two dollars per drink). Like pilgrims to Ernest's drinking shrine, all tourists seem required to pay their respects here. Art exhibitions are held down the street at the **Centro Cultural Wilfredo Lam** (at the corner of San Ignacio), named for Cuba's top modern artist. Books, manuscripts, and photographs of the country's best-known novelist are housed inside the **Centro de Promoción Cultural Alejo Carpentier** (Empedrado, 215).

Plaza de Armas

Plaza de Armas, which surrounds a statue of the patriot Céspedes and is ringed by shaded marble benches and second-hand booksellers, is Havana's oldest square. It dates to the city's founding in 1519.

On the square's eastern side a small neoclassical temple, **El Templete,** marks the spot where the first Catholic mass

Things have changed very little since Hemingway glanced out at this view from his room at the Hotel Ambos Mundos.

was celebrated in 1519. Next door is one of the city's most luxurious hotels, Hotel Santa Isabel. The squat but angular and moated **Castillo de la Real Fuerza** (Fort of the Royal Forces), to the north, is one of the oldest forts in the Americas, begun in 1558. The battlements afford good views over the harbor, and there are craft shops upstairs. The bronze *La Giraldilla* weather vane on one of the fort's towers—depicting a woman scanning the seas for her lost husband, an early Cuban governor—has been adopted as the symbol of the city and of Havana Club rum.

In 1791 the seat of government and the governor's (or captain general's) residence were transferred from the fort to the newly built, baroque **Palacio de los Capitanes Generales** (Palace of the Captain Generals) on the square's western flank. A magnificent structure that was the presidential palace

> "My mojitos at La Bodeguita, my daiquiris at El Floridita"—a personal declaration of drinks and where to have them, attributed to Ernest Hemingway.

and then the municipal palace until Castro seized power, it now houses the **Museo de la Ciudad de la Habana** (the Museum of the City of Havana). Beyond the serene courtyard and its statue of Columbus lie a succession of splendid marbled and chandeliered rooms, some housing old cannonballs and coaches, others decked out in gilded furnishings. The most hallowed room commemorates Cuba's 19th-century independence wars, with the very first Cuban flag and venerated personal objects from generals of the day.

Calle Obispo

Running all the way from Plaza de Armas to Parque Central, the pedestrian-only **Calle Obispo** is Old Havana's most important thoroughfare. Here you can peer into apothecaries unchanged since the 19th century as well as some of Havana's oldest homes. Equally fascinating are the two parallel, partly residential streets —O'Reilly and Obrapía—where grand neoclassical and colonial buildings intermingle with decrepit tenements.

Much of restored Old Havana is concentrated in only a few blocks at the eastern end of these streets. On the corner of Mercaderes and Obispo is the recently renovated, 1920s-era **Hotel Ambos Mundos;** Hemingway lived on and off in room 511 for a couple of years during the 1930s. The room contains original artifacts from Hemingway's many years in Cuba, including the typewriter he used to write most of *For Whom the Bell Tolls* (those not staying in the hotel can visit the room for US$2).

> Cuban addresses usually include the street followed by a number. Helpful hints are *"e/Calles"* ("between the streets") or *"esq."* ("corner of").

Nearby are several museums worth visiting as much for the glorious colonial mansions that house them as for their contents. On Calle Obrapía, between Mercaderes and San Ignacio, is the striking lemon-yellow **Casa de la Obra Pía.** This 17th-century architectural wonder features baroque additions around a flower-drenched courtyard and a full set of beautifully furnished domestic rooms. The owner, a member of one of Cuba's most important families, rescued orphan girls and took them into his home—his *obra pía* (work of piety) that lends its name to both the house and its street. The massive mansion opposite, nearly as impressive, houses the **Casa de África,** with pelts, drums, costumes, carved figures, and furniture from some 26 African countries, as well as a tantalizing collection of objects related to *santería,* the syncretic Afro-Cuban religion (see page 26) and various items related to the period of slavery in Cuba, such as manacles and traps.

The **Museo Numismático** (Calle Oficios, 8) has a comprehensive set of Cuban coins and banknotes. A little farther on lies the **Casa de los Árabes** (Calle Oficios, 12), a Moorish-style 17th-century building that now comprises a bazaar piled high with carpets, robes, and pottery; Havana's only place of worship for Muslims; and a lovely restaurant tucked away in the courtyard.

The streets of Havana are a living museum of chrome-finned wondercars imported during Detroit's heyday, but several that once belonged to pivotal Cuban figures—among them a 1918 Ford truck used by Fidel's father and Che's 1960 Chevrolet Bel Air—are lined up in the **Museo de Autos Antiguos** (Calle Oficios, 13).

Continuing west along Calle Oficios, you'll come to a splendidly restored square, Plaza de San Francisco, with upscale shops, restaurants, and the imposing 18th-century **Iglesia y Convento de San Francisco de Asís.** The convent contains a museum with Spanish treasures, and you can climb the belltower for spectacular views of Old Havana. Concerts are frequently held here. Nearby, you'll find several impeccable colonial-era houses with brilliantly colored façades.

The backstreets around the Plaza Vieja are notable for their dilapidated charm.

Plaza Vieja

Follow charming Calle Mercaderes to the fascinating and aptly named **Plaza Vieja** (Old Square), which began life in 1584 housing wealthy merchants. It is slowly receiving a massive facelift, with assistance from UNESCO, but most of its mansions remain in terrible disrepair. Laundry adorns disintegrating balconies, while in the center of the plaza an incongruous, neoclassical gleaming marble fountain has been installed (it's an unmitigated disaster in this atmospheric corner of Old Havana). On the southwest corner of the square, a fine 18th-century palace has been converted into an arts center. Just east is the Art Nouveau–style, fabulously decayed Hotel Palacio Vienna, a ghost building if ever there was one.

The old backstreets here are full of character but seldom visited by tourists. Down Calle Cuba, between Sol and Luz, stands the 17th century **Convento de Santa Clara,** an expansive com-

plex that takes up several blocks. Inside is a tranquil courtyard garden full of exotic trees. A convent until 1919, it is now an architectural conservation center. It is also a hostel, Residencia Académica Santa Clara, which provides peaceful, simple rooms (see page 128); a lot of visitors have long-term stays on their minds.

The design of the Capitolio was based on that of the Washington D.C. structure.

By the train station, between Calles Picota and Egido, is the modest **Casa Natal de José Martí** (at Calle Leonor Pérez, 314), the birthplace of poet and statesman José Martí. The numerous personal effects on display leave no doubt about Martí's importance in the pantheon of Cuban heroes: he is Cuba's founding father. The train station itself is fascinating, with hundreds of people waiting in line and a parking lot full of bicycle-driven pedicabs and vintage taxis.

The Prado

West of the oldest sections and intimate streets of Old Havana is an area of wide boulevards and grand palaces. The loveliest avenue, the **Prado** (formally known as *Paseo de Martí*), runs from Parque Central to the sea. Grand but run-down buildings, with fading flamingo-pink and lime-green façades and ornate columns, flank a raised promenade of laurels, gas lamps, and marble benches. In the 19th century this was the city's most fashionable strolling ground. Now it serves as a minipark for *habaneros* (as Havana's citizens are called), from coupling lovers and children playing on home-made skateboards to parading prostitutes.

The streets Brasil and Obrapía lead directly west to the monumental **Capitolio,** a replica of the American capitol in Washington, D.C. Completed in 1929, it reflects the period when Cuba was in the thrall of the United States. Its vast bronze doors pictorially chart the island's history, and the immense main gallery inside has a diamond in the floor beneath the dome, symbolizing that now-distant era when Cuba was rich.

Directly behind the Capitolio is the large **Partagás Tobacco Factory,** the biggest export factory in the country—with more than 200 rollers churning out 5 million cigars a year—and one of Havana's top tourist draws. This factory, which has been rolling out *puros* since the mid-19th century, is the best (and, with an admission fee of US$10, the most expensive) to visit on the island; it also has an excellent tobacco shop and smoking lounge for *aficionados* and wannabes. There are two tours daily (see page 81). If the cigars inside strike you as too expensive, you'll have plenty of opportunity to purchase fake or stolen stogies outside the factory, as every third person whispers "You want cigar?" as you pass.

Just east of the Capitolio, on Parque Central near the classic Hotel Inglaterra, stands the magnificent **Gran Teatro,** built in 1837. The home of the Cuban National Ballet and Opera drips with ornate balustrades, shutters, and sculpted columns. The cavernous interior is hardly less awesome but can only be visited during performances.

Those with the Hemingway bug shouldn't miss a visit to **El Floridita** (see page 41), at the intersection of Calles Obispo and Montserrate, one block east of Parque Central. The writer immortalized the swanky bar in *Islands in the Stream.* Hemingway photos adorn the walls, his seat is on the extreme left of the elegant mahogany bar, and his favorite daiquiri is now referred to as the "Papa Hemingway," with double rum and no sugar (everyone knows he was an alcoholic; the barmen claim he was also diabetic). If you don't mind sipping a $6 daiquiri (the monthly

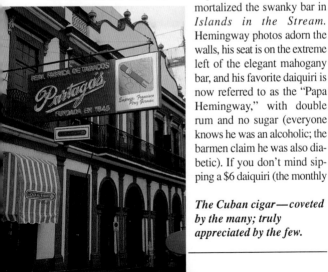

The Cuban cigar — coveted by the many; truly appreciated by the few.

wage of the doorman), the place is eminently capable of evoking the kind of hedonistic refuge expat writers adore.

Ernie and Graham: Literary Footprints

Ernest Hemingway's literary and personal footprints are as deep in Cuba as they are in Spain, and they've become part of the tourist fabric in both places. Hemingway wrote two books based in Cuba, *The Old Man and The Sea and Islands in the Stream*, and in large part he wrote *For Whom the Bell Tolls* (about the Spanish Civil War) from his hotel room in Havana. He was an island resident for two decades.

Pilgrims can trace his life in Cuba at various sights, including Finca Vigía, Cojímar, El Floridita, La Bodeguita del Medio, and the Hotel Ambos Mundos. Despite chummy photos with Castro (they met at the annual Hemingway Fishing Tournament, which Fidel won), the writer's views on the revolution are elusive, although all Cubans accept him as a fervent supporter. It is certain that he identified with the Cuban people. Hemingway abandoned Cuba in 1960 and committed suicide shortly thereafter in Idaho.

Graham Greene's classic novel about Cuban intrigue, *Our Man in Havana*, was first published in 1958. Not only is it an evocative portrait of sleazy 1950s Havana, with scenes set in the Nacional and Sevilla hotels and the Tropicana nightclub. It's also eerily prescient, as the hero invents drawings of Soviet weapons hidden in the Cuban countryside. Nuclear weapons were discovered in Cuba in 1962.

Greene was a great supporter of the revolution, praising Castro, the war against illiteracy, the lack of racial segregation, and the support of the arts. When he went to Cuba to do research for the book in 1958, he took supplies for Castro, who was secluded in the Sierra Maestra, in exchange for an interview that never took place. Greene's support wavered, though, when he learned of the revolution's forced labor camps in the 1960s.

Couples canoodle and swoon in the sea air while strolling along the romantic promenade at Havana's Malecón.

Housed in the grand presidential palace used by presidents (and dictators) between 1920 and 1959, the fascinating and didactic **Museo de la Revolución** is the country's largest and most interesting museum. You'll find an exhaustive exhibit of the trajectory of the 1959 Cuban Revolution, so allow a couple of hours to view it. The most absorbing sections chart the struggle to power with a variety of illustrations: countless maps, evocative photos of both torture victims and triumphal scenes, and assorted personal memorabilia from passports to bloodstained clothes. In the square outside is the ordinary-looking *Granma,* the boat that carried Castro's 81 rebels to shore in 1956; it is now enclosed in glass and guarded by military police.

On the seafront (at Cárcel, 1) the **Museo Nacional de la Música** (National Music Museum) is of interest mainly for its extensive, informative collection of African drums and the many stringed instruments used in Cuban traditional music.

Havana's Forts

Cuba's most impressive forts sit brooding over the capital's commercial harbor. Take a taxi through the road tunnel underneath the water to reach them. The older one, constructed at the end of the 16th century, is the **Castillo de los Tres Santos Reyes Magos del Morro,** better known as "El Morro." From its position at the harbor mouth, the views of Havana over the defiant cannons are magical.

The vast **Fortaleza de San Carlos de la Cabaña** (known as "La Cabaña"), running beside the harbor, was constructed after the English capture of Havana in 1763. The largest fort ever built in the Americas, it is impressively well preserved, and the gardens and ramparts are romantically lit in the evening. A ceremony at 9pm re-enacts the firing of a cannon that marked the closing of the city gates.

New Havana

The walls surrounding Old Havana were razed during the 19th century to allow the city to expand westward. The long, curvaceous, and crumbling **Malecón** (breakwater), a six-lane highway alongside the city's north shore, links the districts of

Taking Foreigners for a Ride

Although many private car owners (*particulares*) operate as freelance taxis, it is illegal for them to take foreigners, as it is for any pedicabs (*bicitaxis*) that don't pay special, higher taxes allowing them to take tourists. If you hire an unlicensed vehicle and are stopped by the police, the driver faces a large fine, though nothing will happen to you. Since the fines are great, you should choose to ride in official vehicles only. Similarly, unlicensed private accommodations (*casas particulares*) face very stiff penalties, so you should at the least be very discreet if you stay at or eat in one.

Those looking for the artsy side of Havana shouldn't miss colorful Calle Hamel.

Central Havana and Vedado. The victim of harmful salt spray, the seafront drive is now more a seafront dive. At its eastern end, primary-colored buildings—a showcase of tragic splendor—seem to fall apart before your eyes. Havana's youth congregate along the Malecón on fine evenings, flying kites, necking, swimming off the rocks, and setting out to sea in giant inner tubes to fish.

Although most visitors will want to concentrate on historic and museum-like Old Havana, the newer districts provide a fascinating view of the areas where most people live and work. The most interesting districts of **New Havana** are Central Havana and Vedado. The former is a congested, lower-middle-class barrio with few attractions for visitors, although a walk along its dusty streets and crumbling façades can be an eye-opening experience. Vedado is the city's principal commercial and residential zone—the epicenter of middle-class Havana—with parks, monuments, hotels, restaurants, theaters, and the University of Havana. Once the stomping grounds of the elite in the 1950s, the "suburb" of Miramar today is home to the offices of rich foreign companies investing in Cuba and the diplomatic missions of foreign governments.

Central Havana (Centro Habana)

Central Havana is a ramshackle residential and commercial area. The city's main shopping street, **Calle San Rafael**, traverses it from the Parque Central westward. This might be Havana at its least guarded. While having a fascinating stroll here, you can stop to have your nails painted, or get a shave and a haircut, all right on the pavement. One of the country's new private markets has overrun Havana's small Chinatown, at Calles Zanja and Rayo. Amazingly, even downtrodden Central Havana is being transformed by the presence of glittering dollar stores.

The neighborhood known as *Cayo Hueso*, just behind the Malecón, is a rough-and-tumble barrio once populated by cigar-factory workers. Today the main reason to visit is to check out **Calle Hamel**, where the artist Salvador González has dedicated himself to preserving the area's Afro-Cuban culture. The small alleyway, the scene of a good many photo shoots, is entirely done over in street art and graffiti. González has his studio here, and on Sundays at around 1pm there are performances of Afro-Cuban ritual and rumba.

Vedado

Vedado had its heyday in the 1940s and 1950s, when such

Be careful never to turn your back on "The Miracle Woman."

Che Guevara's image can be seen throughout Cuba—he is constructed with steel at the Plaza de la Revolución.

gangsters as Meyer Lansky held sway in the Nacional, Riviera, and Capri hotels. Such stars as Frank Sinatra and Ginger Rogers performed, and American tourists emptied their wallets in glittering casinos. The revolution put the lid on the nightlife by banning gambling and deporting the Mafiosi.

Save for the stately, elegant **Hotel Nacional** (see page 129), overlooking the Malecón, the hotels here have now seen better days. Vedado is Havana's most respectable business district as well as a leafy residential area, spacious and orderly in comparison with Old and Central Havana.

Business is centered on **La Rampa,** the name for Calle 23 from Calle L to the sea. Opposite the tower-block Hotel Habana Libre—the Havana Hilton in pre-revolutionary days —is the **Coppelia ice cream park.** At this institution, locals queue for hours for the prized ice cream, eating several scoops

Havana Highlights

Attractions and Sights

Calles Obispo, **O'Reilly**, and **Obra Pía**. Old Havana's atmospheric principal thoroughfares.

Casa Museo de Ernest Hemingway. On the outskirts of Havana is Hemingway's house, full of original furnishings and possessions.

Cementerio de Cristóbal Colón. A colossal cemetery dating from 1868, with fabulously baroque mausoleums.

Malecón. The splendid, down-at-the-heel seafront: prepare to get wet.

"El Morro" and **"La Cabaña"** forts. Great city views from vast colonial strongholds.

Museo de la Revolución. Displays providing a full account of Cuba's revolution, situated in the presidential palace.

Palacio de los Capitanes Generales. The city museum in a baroque palace.

Partagás Tobacco Factory. A massive, busy cigar factory, with daily tours, smoke shop, and smoking lounge.

Plaza de Armas, Plaza de la Catedral, Plaza Vieja. Old Havana's show-piece squares, with glorious colonial buildings.

Eating, Drinking, and Nightlife

La Bodeguita del Medio. Gritty bar renowned for its graffiti-etched walls and splendid *mojitos* (cocktails).

El Floridita. Swank lounge famous for well-documented Hemingway connections and daiquiris.

Hotel Nacional. Havana's grandest hotel—a classic overlooking the malecón.

Tropicana. Famously over-the-top, open-air cabaret with gaily dressed (make that half-dressed) mulatta showgirls galore.

in one sitting or ladling them into saucepans to take home. Hard-hearted foreigners paying in dollars down their scoops in a cordoned-off area. Coppelia was instrumental in the award-winning Cuban film *Fresa y Chocolate* ("Strawberry and Chocolate"), a daring film about freedoms and revolutionary fervor in contemporary Havana (its title is a wry reference to the lack of choices of ice cream flavors—indeed, of all things—in Cuba).

A short walk up the hill brings you to the University of Havana, founded in the early 18th century, a quiet, attractive campus of neoclassical buildings. English-speaking students eager to meet foreigners are numerous here. Directly east on Calle San Miguel, between Calles Ronda and Mazón, is the fine and surprising **Museo Napoleónico.** The mansion boasts not only Empire furniture but also a remarkable collection of Napoleonic memorabilia: busts, portraits, and even his pistol, hat, and death mask from St. Helena. The house and contents were acquired by the state from a rich owner in 1960.

In the same year, the government acquired the **Museo de Artes Decorativas,** at Calle 17 between Calles D and E. Each room in this grand 19th-century villa is furnished in a particular style: English Chippendale, Chinese, baroque, or Art Deco in the fabulous bathroom.

Vedado's top sight, though, is the **Cementerio de Cristóbal Colón** (Columbus Cemetery). Massive marble mausoleums line the principal avenues of the cemetery, a vast city of the dead established in the late 1800s. Cubans come to pray and place flowers at the tomb of La Milagrosa ("The Miracle Worker"), who helps people in need. It is said that she was buried with her infant at her feet, but when their bodies were exhumed, the child was found cradled in her arms.

Plaza de la Revolución

The barren district known as **Plaza de la Revolución** is worth visiting only for a brief glimpse of the square of the same name, a vast concourse where political rallies are held. Hideous high-rise ministry buildings erected in the 1950s by Batista and a giant, tapering concrete obelisk —looking like a rocket launch pad with a pensive José Martí at its foot—provide the scenery. The Ministry of the Interior building, adorned by a giant iron sculpture-mural of Che, is where Fidel Castro supposedly punches the clock.

Musicians share Cuba's rich heritage through the rhythm and melody of the son.

Miramar

More attractive is the exclusive suburb of **Miramar,** to the west. The villas of the pre-revolutionary rich, expropriated by the state, have now been divided into apartments or turned into offices. But embassies along Avenida 5 still imbue the area with a leisurely, privileged feel.

At the corner of Calle 14, the **Museo del Ministerio del Interior** has some intriguing exhibits relating to CIA espionage, including code boxes concealed in briefcases, decoding equipment, and a transmitter hidden in a fake rock. Don't miss the towering Russian Embassy, between Calles 62 and 66, looking for all the world like a giant concrete robot.

Growing as an attraction—literally—is the **Maqueta de Habana** (Calle 28, 113 e/Avenida 1 y 3), a scale model of the entire city in astounding 1:1,000 detail. Havana is so expansive that a visit to the Maqueta can help organize the city's neighborhoods in your mind.

Havana's Outskirts

Havana's suburbs are sprawling and grimy, but they contain a couple of places associated with Ernest Hemingway that are magnets for those seeking to trace the Nobel Prize winner's life in Cuba. From 1939 to 1960 he lived on and off in the Finca Vigía, now the **Casa Museo de Ernest Hemingway.** The sight is 11 km (7 miles) southeast of Havana in San Francisco de Paula, so you will have to take a taxi. Visitors may not enter the graceful bungalow villa, but by peering through windows and doors you can see all the rooms furnished as the writer had them, covered in bullfighting posters and filled with more than 9,000 books, including such titles as *The Guide to Hunting and Fishing in Cuba.* You can roam the lush gardens searching out his motorboat, the *Pilar*.

Hemingway kept the *Pilar* 10 km (6 miles) to the east of Havana at **Cojímar**. Next to a diminutive fort in the little town's old corner is a Hemingway bust, looking out over the bay. The writer frequented La Terraza restaurant nearby (see page 138), worth visiting for its many photographs of Hemingway in action. His captain and cook aboard the *Pilar* was the fisherman Gregorio Fuentes. Until his death at the age of 104 in 2002, Gregorio would regale visitors with tales of his hero. He always denied that he was Santiago, the title character in *The Old Man and the Sea*, but he did not dispute that it was in Cojímar that Hemingway found the inspiration for his famous novel.

Farther east, approximately 18 km (11 miles) from Havana, the **Playas del Este** (Eastern Beaches) are less charming but a big draw for Cubans unable to afford much in the way of beach vacations. These beaches are acceptable for a short break from city life, but you are unlikely to want to spend your holiday here. The long, sandy beaches are excellent but often buffeted by winds.

PINAR DEL RÍO PROVINCE

Due west of Havana is **Pinar del Río province,** Cuba's westernmost region—a finger of land with the Gulf of Mexico to the north and the Caribbean to the south. It contains some of Cuba's most beautiful countryside among the lush Guaniguanico mountains and surrounding patchwork of lushly verdant fields *(vegas),* where the world's finest tobacco is cultivated. In the beautiful Viñales valley, tobacco fields and ancient limestone formations produce spectacular scenery more reminiscent of Southeast Asia than the Caribbean. In

The lush Viñales valley is a prime example of the natural gifts that have been bestowed upon the island of Cuba.

this resolutely agricultural region, oxen tilling red-earth fields and cowboy peasants *(guajiros)* on horseback are much more common than cars. Residents of Havana might think of it as a poor backwater, but the easy, almost somnolent pace, breathtaking countryside, and welcoming residents of Pinar del Río make it one of Cuba's certain highlights.

There are beaches and excellent diving farther west, near **Playa María la Gorda,** but for most visitors the star attractions are the irresistible town of **Viñales** and its beautiful valley. Many visitors take organized daytrips of the region from Havana hotels, but an overnight stay in Viñales—overlooking the valley—is highly recommended.

Start your explorations by driving west on the *autopista* (highway) linking Havana with the province's capital city of Pinar del Río. About 63 km (39 miles) along the highway, a turnoff leaves the level, palm-dotted plains for **Soroa,** where a richly endowed botanical garden nestles in the mountain

foothills near a tired little tourist complex. A guided tour reveals an orchid garden, lychee and mango trees, coffee plants, and splendid specimens of *jagüey* and *ceiba* trees. A restaurant in the villa of Castillo de las Nubes on a nearby mountain has stunning views.

At the end of the highway, 175 km (109 miles) west of

The crude images at the Mural de la Prehistoria date only to the 1960s.

Havana, the small city of **Pinar del Río** is a bustling commercial center. Along the main street, Calle José Martí, low-rise neoclassical buildings in blues, yellows, greens, and orange have a stately but dilapidated quality. In backstreet houses men make homemade cigars; you'll find a small, interesting tobacco factory, **Francisco Donatien Fábrica de Tabacos,** housed in an old jail below the Plaza de la Independencia. Visitors are welcome here and at the less picturesque **Casa Garay Rum Factory,** on Avenida Isabel Rubio, where they make a local rum liqueur called *guayabita del Pinar.*

The road southwest from the city to San Juan y Martínez leads deep into tobacco's heartland—the **Vuelta Abajo**— where the world's greatest tobacco is grown. Amid fields of big green leaves ripening in the sun and plantations covered in canvas sheets stand wooden tobacco barns. Here, leaves are hung on poles with a needle and thread and then dried, turning from green to brown.

Some 27 km (17 miles) to the north of Pinar del Río lies the most picturesque corner of Cuba. The deeply green **Viñales valley** is spattered with *mogotes,* sheer-sided limestone masses covered in thick vegetation. Remnants of an underwater plateau that collapsed in the Jurassic period, they are part of a geological formation at least 150 million years old. Tobacco (of slightly lesser quality than in the Vuelta Abajo) grows here in a patchwork of fields and dries in *bohíos,* constructed with shaggy thatch. Cigar-chomping *guajiros* in enormous straw hats urge on their oxen, while vultures swoop overhead. At any time of day you can wander into the fields and meet the modest farmers, who might smother you with hospitality (cigars, coffee, and so forth) and pose for photos.

At **Casa del Veguero** (Carretera a Viñales, km 25) you'll find the grizzled farmer "El Niño," whom the government has unofficially appointed the face of tobacco—Cuba's Marlboro man. Next to his farm, on the road into Viñales, is a state-owned tobacco and souvenir shop. The best valley views can be had from either of its lovely and economical hotels: Los Jazmines and La Ermita. The sight at dusk is especially alluring.

The town of **Viñales** is surprisingly spruce, with a fetching, arcaded main street and lovely rustic scenes down the back lanes. Next to the *paladar* (a restaurant in a private home) and across from the Cupet gas station is a delightful botanical garden, overseen by two elderly women whose father began planting the hundreds of species of plants.

Nearby, a couple of local tourist sights, on all the package excursions, have curiosity value but little else. One limestone *mogote* just west of town was painted by workmen dangling on ropes in the 1960s with a **Mural de la Prehistoria** (Mural of Prehistory)—commissioned by Castro himself—that is 120 meters (370 feet) high and 180 meters (550 feet) long. The garish painting, an exercise in

Call Me a Camello?

Transportation in Cuba encompasses a wide range of colorful vehicles, such as the following:

guagua	("wah-wah") bus
ómnibus	bus
carro	automobile
colectivo	a vintage American jalopy that functions as a Cuban peso taxi; also called *máquina* ("machine")
coche	horse-drawn cart
camión	truck
camello	a long-bed truck and large-scale people mover (literally a "camel")
bicitaxi	bicycle taxi (pedicab)

bad judgment and sloppy execution, depicts evolution from an ammonite to a dinosaur to advanced (and presumably socialist) *Homo sapiens.* Just to the north of town, the extensive **Cueva del Indio** (Indian Cave) was used as a hideout by Indians after the conquest. A tour through the cave includes a brief ride on an underground river in a boat (which would-be emigrants once stole for an unsuccessful escape attempt to Florida). Both mural and cave have decent tourist restaurants. About 4 km (2.5 miles) north of Viñales, the **Cueva del Viñales** is a curious bar and disco carved out of a cave; amazingly, it's open 24 hours.

Laze in the tropical calm of Cayo Largo—a far cry from the hectic city pace.

Cayo Largo and the Isle of Youth

The two main islands in the Archipiélago de los Canarreos, south of western Cuba, could not be more different. Cayo Largo is a tourist enclave where visitors are never more than a few yards from sugar-white sands. Yet it's an antiseptic place, devoid of any Cubans except those who work there. By contrast, the Isle of Youth sees virtually no tourists except those at the rather isolated Hotel El Colony (on the small island's southwestern tip), who come exclusively for the superb diving at a nearby beach.

Cayo Largo, an island 25 km (15.5 miles) long and the most easterly of the Archipiélago de los Canarreos, might be your Caribbean paradise—if all you're looking for is a dazzling white beach and clear blue seas. Other than the miles of beaches, there's not much else of consequence here except mangrove, scrub, and half a dozen comfortable hotels with a full program of entertainment and watersports. Turtles nest in the sand at one end of the island. At the other you can go sailing, diving, or deep-sea fishing or take a boat trip to **Playa Sirena,** an incomparable strip of sand a 10-minute boat ride away, where lobster lunches are available. Cayo Largo, with its captive tourist audience, is considerably more expensive than the mainland.

Some package tourists spend the whole of their holiday on Cayo Largo. Those with low boredom thresholds might consider coming for only a daytrip or for overnight trips on half-hour flights from Havana and Varadero.

The **Isla de la Juventud (Isle of Youth)** is Cuba's largest offshore island, some 50 km (31 miles) in diameter, but not its prettiest. It is said to have been the location for Robert Louis Stevenson's *Treasure Island;* pirates once buried their booty here. The island received its jaunty name in the 1970s, when as many as 22,000 foreign students (mainly from politically sympathetic African countries) studied here in no fewer than 60 schools.

The island fails to live up to its colorful past. The number of foreign students has dropped to fewer than 5,000, and derelict boarding schools dot the monotonous countryside. However, there are plenty of virgin beaches to be discovered, and in a slightly dingy cave at **Punta del Este** you can examine enigmatic symbols painted centuries ago by Siboney Indians.

For more accessible entertainment, **Nueva Gerona,** the island's little capital, is moderately attractive, with striped

Varadero offers the resort lifestyle, but doesn't really serve up an authentic view of Cuban life.

awnings along its smart, pillared main street. Just east of town, the **Presidio Modelo** (Model Prison) is fascinating. The dictator Machado built this copy of an American penitentiary in 1931. Castro and 26 of his rebels were sent here after the storming of the Moncada Barracks; their ward and the cell in which Castro was kept in solitary confinement have been reconstructed.

MATANZAS PROVINCE

The province east of Havana—largely flat sugar-cane country—was in the 19th century Cuba's most important cane-producing region. For today's visitors, however, the focus is on the big-time beach resort of Varadero, Cuba's biggest draw, with opportunities for side trips to atmospheric, time-warped towns and to the swamplands of the south coast.

Varadero

Varadero has enthusiastic proponents and equally passionate detractors among its visitors. A long peninsula with many dozens of hotels and restaurants, bars, fast-food cafés, and grocery shops (and more of each on the way), Varadero doesn't feel much like Cuba at all. The easy-spending gringos here stick out like a sore thumb in this land of hardship, and their isolation increases year after year. Varadero is a package destination, and plenty of visitors fly into it and never leave. If you want to see and learn what makes Cuba a fascinating place, though, you'll need to escape for at least a couple of daytrips. In towns around Cuba you'll meet tourists who—like jailbird escapees—rejoice at having gotten out of Varadero.

Still, there are plenty of delighted folks for whom this is heaven: a 20-km (12-mile) long, virtually uninterrupted white-sand beach with shallow, clean waters that are described immodestly by the authorities as the most beautiful in the world. Varadero isn't a recent development by a government desperate for hard currency (though officials are determined to see it become a faceless cash cow not unlike Cancún). It was in the 1920s that Varadero first attracted millionaires, who built palatial holiday villas. Tourism proper began after World War II with the construction of casinos and such establishments as the Hotel Internacional.

Even the beach, Varadero's best feature, can be problematic. Northern winds kick up with considerable frequency, and lifeguards put out the red flags to warn of the dangerous undertow. There is often a strong smell from the oil pumps on the resort's outskirts. Prostitution and hassling are constant and blatant, and other pests (namely, mosquitoes) are a real annoyance. Moreover, the resort is spread out over 17 km (11 miles), with no real center, so you need transport to get around.

On the other hand, Varadero has many very comfortable hotels (most of them the results of international joint ventures), open bars, and an excellent range of watersports. And, unlike other parts of Cuba, topless sunbathing is allowed here. If you tire of the beach, there are organized excursions to every conceivable point of interest on the island—including Havana, an hour and a half away.

Varadero occupies a long, thin insular spit of sand, with water on both sides and a bridge to the mainland. Between Calles 25 and 54 there's something of a local community of Cubans, with ancient Cadillacs parked outside rickety wooden bungalows. The liveliest area is around Calles 54 to 64, with a shopping mall, a host of restaurants and bars, and the **Retiro Josone,** a pretty park set around a palm-fringed boating lake.

Spreading several miles farther east are the newest hotel complexes and also the restaurant **Las Américas,** an opulent beachside mansion completed by the French millionaire Irenée Du Pont in 1930.

Matanzas and Cárdenas

Though just spitting distance away, these quintessentially Cuban towns are a world apart from Varadero. Their poorly stocked shops, dusty backstreets, and primitive transport provide Varadero's package tourists with a con-

An ancient chemist's shop displays over one hundred years of pharmaceuticals.

venient insight into everyday Cuban life before they're whisked back to their hotels.

Matanzas, 42 km (26 miles) west of Varadero, is busy and grimy. Lying alongside a deep bay, it came into its own during the 19th century as the country's sugar capital. On the leafy main square, Parque Libertad, the **Museo Farmacéutico** is a wonderfully preserved chemist's shop, founded in 1882. On a street running east toward the bay, the **Catedral de San Carlos** is notable for its many murals, some restored, some badly in need of attention.

> *"Playa Girón: La Primera Derrota del Imperialismo en América Latina"* ("The First Defeat of Imperialism in Latin America")—billboard at Bay of Pigs.

A little farther to the east, impressive buildings on Plaza de la Vigía include the **Palacio de Junco,** which houses a second-rate provincial museum, and the **Teatro Sauto.** Constructed in 1863, the lovely theater has tiers of wrought-iron boxes and a mural ceiling; there are performances most weekends.

Las Cuevas de Bellamar, a short distance to the south, are Cuba's oldest tourist site. The caves were discovered by chance in 1861 by a Chinese slave. Tours (in English) take you down into a vast chamber for views of the many stalactites and stalagmites.

Fortunes have changed—and not for the better—for the town of **Cárdenas,** 15 km (9 miles) east of Varadero. Once the island's most important port for sugar exportation, it's now a ramshackle place with long shopping lines and dozens of horses and carts streaming up and down its main street. With its statue of Columbus, the main square is elegant, and the **Museo Oscar María de Rojas** (at Avenida 4 and Calle 12) houses a quirky, varied collection of items, from slaves' manacles to a 19th-century funeral coach and two fleas all dressed up to dance.

Zapata Peninsula

The **Zapata Peninsula** is the largest wetlands area in the Caribbean, flat as a pancake and covered in mangrove swamps and grassland plains. Its protected wildlife includes crocodiles, manatees, and numerous species of birds. Frankly, though, you are unlikely to see any interesting wildlife unless you take a guided bird-watching trip from **Playa Larga.** You can see penned reptiles at the crocodile farm at **La Boca,** a popular tourist site where you can pose with a baby croc and taste crocodile steak.

A more appealing prospect is picturesque **Guamá,** a half-hour boat ride from La Boca along an artificial channel and then across the vast **Laguna del Tesoro** (Treasure Lake). Legend has it that the Indians dumped their jewels into the water rather than surrender them to Spanish *conquistadores.* Guamá is a group of tiny islands connected by wooden bridges. A few visitors stay in the thatched *cabañas* (see page 131), but most just come to wander along the boardwalk, greet the ducks and egrets, and have a meal.

The peninsula is best known, however, for its bloody role in clandestine political warfare. South of La Boca you soon come to Playa Girón—site of the 1961 US-led **Bay of Pigs** invasion (see page 19). At irregular intervals

American dollars (not pesos) will buy a whole host of Cuban souvenirs.

The majestic Sierra del Escambray rise in the distance behind the settlement of Trinidad.

along the often crab-infested road are concrete memorials to those who died during the invasion. There are two simple, isolated bungalow hotel complexes on the bay, one at quiet **Playa Larga,** the other at **Playa Girón,** where the already scruffy beach is further spoiled by a concrete breakwater. One major attraction, however, is the excellent **Museo Playa Girón,** which serves as an emotional memorial to the three-day Bay of Pigs debacle.

CENTRAL CUBA

Tourists, usually eager to get to one end of the country or the other, usually whiz through central Cuba. The only tourist beacons are on or near the coasts: in the south around Cienfuegos's bay and at Trinidad (a gorgeous colonial gem) and in the north at the small resorts of Cayo Coco and Guillermo and Playa Santa Lucía. Elsewhere, those who pause to explore can feel like goldfish in a bowl—foreigners are still a novelty here.

Central Cuba comprises five provinces: from west to east these are Cienfuegos, Villa Clara, Sancti Spiritus, Ciego de Avila, and Camagüey. Each focuses on a provincial city of the same or similar name, typically of some interest yet not likely to detain you for longer than a day. The west has the best scenery, found in the lush Sierra del Escambray mountains. To the east of Sancti Spiritus, towns are plunked down on unremittingly flat plains. Here, sugar cane as high as three men grows in abundance, trucks trundle around with monster bundles of the stuff, and chimneys of sugar-cane factories poke skyward like cathedral towers. In Camagüey, the cattle-ranch province, rusty watermills punctuate the skyline and *vaqueros* (cowboys) slouch on horses with machetes and lassos at the ready.

Cienfuegos

The best feature of the port city of **Cienfuegos** (250 km/155 miles southeast of Havana) is its position, set at the back of a large bay. Despite the industry on its periphery, the center is quite attractive, with pastel-colored neoclassical buildings. Many travelers now stop off here on their way to Trinidad.

The focal point in town is **Parque José Martí,** one of the grandest squares in the country. Here you will find the monumental red-domed government offices, an early 19th-century cathedral with a startling gold-painted interior, and a music hall *(casa de la trova;* see page 82) with whimsical flourishes. Take a guided tour of the town's finest colonial building, the **Teatro Tomás Terry,** on the north side of the square. Built in 1890, it was named after a rich sugar plantation owner from Venezuela. The interior, largely original, has a lovely frescoed ceiling and a semicircle of tiered boxes and wooden seats. Enrico Caruso and Sara Bernhardt once performed here, and

Trinidad's colonial history is memorialized at the Museo de Arquitectura Trinitaria.

on weekends you may be able to catch a performance by one of Cuba's top ballet companies. The **Catedral de la Purísima Concepción,** built in 1870, is on the east side of the square. It has an attractive interior with French stained-glass windows depicting the twelve apostles.

The Prado is the town's principal thoroughfare, a palm-lined boulevard that takes you down to the spit of land protruding into the bay past smart waterside villas. At the edge of Punta Gorda, near the end of the Malecón (Calle 37), is the **Palacio del Valle.** This ornate palace, now a restaurant, was finished in 1917; its ceilings and walls are covered in patterned stonework.

At the mouth of the bay, on the western side, the **Castillo de Jagua** was constructed by the Spanish in 1732 (long before the city's founding in 1819) to ward off pirates. You reach the castle on a tiny ferry from the Hotel Pasacaballo on the eastern side of the bay. Close to the hotel is the best beach in the area, **Playa Rancho Luna.**

The **Jardín Botánico Soledad,** 18 km (11 miles) outside Cienfuegos on the road to Trinidad, is the oldest botanical garden in Cuba (it dates to 1899) and one of the finest tropical gardens in the world. Ask at the tourist office in Cienfuegos about guided tours of the gardens.

Trinidad

The scenic, undulating 80-km (50-mile) road east from Cienfuegos to Trinidad skirts the foothills of the Sierra del Escambray, Cuba's second-highest mountain range. The beguiling town of **Trinidad,** the third of Diego Velázquez's original seven settlements, subsequently became rich through the smuggling, slave, and sugar trades. Its sizable old town is endowed with marvelous Spanish colonial architecture and has been named by UNESCO as a "World Heritage Site." Cuba could package it as a time capsule: it is the island's prettiest town and one of the finest preserved colonial cities in all the Americas.

Within easy striking distance of Trinidad are enough attractions to make a longer stay especially rewarding, including the fine beach of Playa Ancón, the lush Valley of the Sugar Mills, and waterfalls and treks in the Escambray mountains.

Carefully restored mansions of the well-to-do have been turned into museums, while art galleries, craft shops, and restaurants occupy additional lovely old buildings. No traffic, not even bicycles, can cope well with Trinidad's wildly uneven, cobbled street surfaces, so peace reigns—especially before and after the tour-bus hordes arrive. Few telltale signs of the 20th century have, as yet, encroached on this wonderfully somnolent outpost. At night the old town is coffin-quiet. For the tranquillity alone, it is worth staying one night or more in Trinidad.

The old town clusters around the Plaza Mayor, an incomparably pretty square of painted railings, fanciful urns, greyhound statues, and bright colonial buildings. To the left of the comparatively plain church, Iglesia de la Santísima Trinidad, the **Museo Romántico** with its collections of fine furniture and porcelain. The square's two other little museums both have attractive courtyards and cool interiors. The **Museo de Arqueología** exhibits bones of Indians and slaves along with a few stuffed animals, while the **Museo de Arquitectura Colonial** has examples of woodwork, ironwork, stained glass, and other items culled from colonial houses in town.

To Bring or Not to Bring: Assistance

Cubans are in dire need of many consumer and health-related products, and tourists often bring expensive (or hard-to-find) items to give as gifts. A debate rages among travelers about whether this is an act of kindness or gross paternalism, an act that teaches Cubans to expect material goods from foreigners or, worse, to beg. Some visitors take gifts only to those who welcome them into their homes.

Whatever your position on the issue, Cubans might appreciate the following: toothpaste, diapers, soap, aspirin, lipstick, pens, and pencils. In some cases, it's a good idea to take school supplies to schools, so that supplies can be distributed evenly among children.

Beach bunnies beware—Playa Ancón might capture your heart with its pristine sands and offshore reef.

A block north of the Plaza Mayor is the **Museo Nacional de la Lucha Contra Bandidos** (National Museum of the Struggle against the Bandits), housed in a former convent. The bandits in question were counter-revolutionary rebels who hid in the Escambray mountains during the 1960s. The stupendous 360-degree view from the yellow belltower (a landmark) is the big draw.

A block south of Plaza Mayor on Calle Simón Bolivar stands the grand Palacio Cantero, built in 1830. Painted pillars, scrolls, shells, pediments, and drapes embellish the interior, eclipsing the historical artifacts and old furniture that now form the **Museo Municipal de Historia.** It has its own fine tower, though climbing its rickety narrow steps can be a trial if a group has arrived there first.

The tiny **Piro Guinart cigar factory** (on Maceo at the corner of Colón) has only about 30 hand rollers and allows vistors to take a peek inside. A block south of the Plaza Mayor are two streets completely given over to sellers of handmade lace and other crafts.

Aimless wandering is especially fruitful in Trinidad—and, since dozens of street names have changed and neither maps nor residents seem sure of what to call many of them, roaming without a plan is the only practical solution. Virtually every street is its own colonial treasure and feast for the eyes. Near the bus station, you might stumble across the musical septet "Los Pinos" jamming in the street, just out of reach of kids playing stickball. Farther afield, southeast along Calle J. M. Márquez, you'll find **Ermita de Santa Ana,** a bricked-up church overlooking the town on a hill where boys fly homemade kites.

Around Trinidad

Trinidad's prosperity in the 19th century came from the fruits of 50 sugar mills nearby in the scenic **Valle de los Ingenios** (Valley of the Sugar Mills), like Trinidad a UNESCO "World

Go on down to the swimmin' hole—spend a day of aquatic bliss beneath the waterfall in Topes de Collantes.

Heritage Site." A *mirador* (lookout) with spectacular views is just 5 km (3 miles) out of town. Just 10 km (6 miles) farther east is the Manacas-Iznaga, where you can explore a lovely colonial hacienda house and its startling, rocket-shaped **Torre de Manacas-Iznaga.** From the top of the tower, the Iznaga family would keep watch over their slaves toiling in the fields. If you don't have a car, you can hire a private taxi for about US$12 roundtrip. A special 18th-century steam train used in the sugar trade traverses the whole valley for tourists; if it is functioning, it is a must. The train leaves from Estación Dragones, 1 km (⅝ mile) from the city center, at 10am and returns at noon.

Beach worshippers should head to **Playa Ancón,** about 16 km (10 miles) from Trinidad, an excellent strip of white sand and clear waters. Here you'll find diving at an offshore coral reef, a good choice of watersports, and two hotels popular with package tourists. Again, you can hire a taxi or pick up a bicycle rental (give it a test ride first, as many are so primitive that they would be scoffed at by any self-respecting commuter from Hanoi or Beijing). Another good beach and fishing excursion, offered by Rumbos Tours, is the daytrip to the tiny island of **Cayo Blanco** from Playa Ancón.

Sierra del Escambray

More compact than the eastern and western ranges on the island, the **Sierra del Escambray** (Escambray mountains), coated in luxuriant vegetation, are arguably Cuba's most beautiful range and easily accessible. Blessed with their own microclimate, the mountains are a blessedly cool refuge from Trinidad.

To get to the **Topes de Collantes** national park, take the road west of Trinidad for the steep 15-km (9-mile) climb through dense forests of palms, eucalyptus, and pines. You'll pass a health resort, a Stalinesque complex that boasts decent facilities but lacks life. Like rewards at the end of excellent day hikes, there are two beautiful waterfalls: Salto de Caburní, at 62 m (203 ft), and Salto Vega Grande. Wear sturdy shoes, as each is a steep trek of 4 km (2.5 miles) along a narrow and often muddy trail. You can swim in the chilly natural pools underneath the falls. For Caburní, park at the graffiti-infested Casa de Gallo and hit the trail nearby. Jeep excursions can be hired (US$25 per person) at the Rumbos tourism office in Trinidad (Calle Simón Bolívar, 430). There's a US$4 admission fee just beyond the Kurhotel health resort.

Sancti Spiritus

Few tourists make it to this provincial capital, and it isn't likely to detain you for more than a couple of hours. Approximately 80 km (50 miles) east of Trinidad is **Sancti Spiritus,** one of Velázquez's seven original townships. However, it's only likely to entertain you for an hour or two.

From the town's pleasant Plaza Sánchez, wander two blocks south to the main sight, **Iglesia Parroquial Mayor de Espíritu Santo.** This venerable, towered church has foundations from 1522, making it the country's oldest (though the present stone church in fact was built in 1680). Nearby is the **Puente Yayabo,** an early 19th-century bridge that recalls Romanesque bridges in Europe. From the river take the lovely, twisting street **Calle Llano,** a cobblestoned affair festooned with graceful colonial houses in soft pastels and iron grilles. The nearby **Museo de Arte Colonial** (Calle Plácido Sur, 74) is an 18th-century palace with two peaceful courtyards and a succession of grandly furnished rooms suffused with a gentle light entering through stained-glass windows.

Cayo Coco and Cayo Guillermo

These offshore cays—budding starlets of Cuban joint-tourism initiatives with foreign companies—are reached by a road carving through pineapple orchards and the town of Morón, which is not as idiotically named as you might think. The road becomes a causeway across the Bahía de Perros; it's so long (28 km/17 miles) that you can't see the land at the far end as you set off.

Cayo Coco is named not for coconuts but for a bird: the ibis, as revealed in Hemingway's *Islands in the Stream.* The author patrolled these shores in World War II on the lookout for Nazis. Ibises and other wading birds, often pink flamingoes, can be seen balancing in the brackish waters around the principal causeway

A sunset like this will make you fall in love — with enchanting Cayo Guillermo.

and a smaller causeway connecting the cay to **Cayo Guillermo.**

It's the superb, impossibly white sandy beaches, the intensely blue waters, and the excellent fishing that draw travelers, and there's not much else to distract you. Both cays are covered in forest or thick undergrowth, and there are no settlements whatsoever (the only Cubans who visit are workers). Plans are afoot to build hotels all along the 22 km (14 miles) of shell-shaped beaches on Cayo Coco, but accommodations are currently limited. A wide range of non-motorized watersports are available to hotel guests; diving and safaris are popular. Cayo Guillermo's single hotel offers a similar gamut of watersports alongside the shallowest of waters. If you hire a moped or Jeep from either hotel, there are virgin beaches to discover.

Camagüey

About 550 km (342 miles) southeast of Havana, **Camagüey** is a bustling but attractive and comfortable colonial city; its population of 300,000 is Cuba's third largest. Restrained old façades hide picturesque courtyards, and there are some half-dozen squares, each boasting a crumbling and still functioning old church.

The cattle-grazed plains of the province of Camagüey hold little water, so long ago the citizens fashioned enormous earthenware pots to catch and store rainwater. Called *tinajones,* these still adorn many squares and courtyard patios.

The city's most famous son, a general from the Ten Years' War, was born in 1841 at the **Casa Natal de Ignacio Agramonte,** a handsome, early 19th-century mansion in the city center on Plaza de los Trabajadores. The patriot is remembered through personal effects; he met his death in battle in 1873. Visit **La Merced** church

opposite to see peeling frescoes and the venerated objects stored in the crypt.

A dashing equine statue of Agramonte forms the centerpiece of **Parque Agramonte,** just to the south. The cathedral occupies one side of the park, and the Casa de la Trova (see page 82), around a floral patio, features musical performances afternoon and evening.

Visitors looking for a quiet getaway will adore the old world charm of Camagüey.

A ten-minute walk west down Calle Cristo brings you to a dignified 18th-century church, **Santo Cristo del Buen Viaje** (Christ of Good Travels), perfectly named for out-of-town visitors. Behind the church is a great sea of crosses and marble saints in a picturesque cemetery; church officials claim it is wholly unrelated to travels that didn't go so well. A few blocks north is the **Convento de Nuestra Señora del Carmen**. Dating from the early 19th century, the church facade is one of the most beautiful in Cuba and is unique in Camagüey for having two towers. It has recently been restored to its former splendor.

Camagüey's finest feature—and marvelously restored—is **Plaza San Juan de Dios,** an angular old cobblestoned square surrounded by brightly hued, single-story buildings dating from the 18th century plus a lovely yellow church alongside a restored former hospital. It's one of Cuba's most beautiful plazas. A few blocks south, near the river, is an impressive agricultural market open every day and stocked with a surprising surfeit of meat and produce.

Playa Santa Lucía

An hour-and-a-half drive (110 km/68 miles) from Camagüey on the north coast, remote **Playa Santa Lucía** beckons sun worshippers with resort hotels strung along a particularly fine peninsular strip of sand. Each hotel backs directly onto the beach. A superb coral reef lies offshore, and diving here is excellent. Aside from a couple of roadside bars, however, nightlife is limited to hotel entertainment. The only other drawback is the mosquitoes, as voracious as anywhere on the island.

To counter the isolation of Playa Santa Lucía, the tourist authorities offer a wide range of excursions, including a rodeo at Rancho King, deep-sea fishing, and boat and helicopter trips for days on the beach at such unspoiled cays as Cayo Sabinal and Cayo Saetía. A bus service visits **Playa Los Cocos,** some 5 km (3 miles) away; with sheltered aquamarine waters, it's a strong contender for the title of "Cuba's most beautiful beach." Adjacent is La Boca, a very small community of waterside shacks with fish restaurants.

ORIENTE: THE EAST

Prior to the revolution, the east of Cuba was a single province known simply as **Oriente** ("East"), and most Cubans still refer to the region with this name.

> As resorts go, the name "Guardalavaca" does not forebode a whole lot of excitement. It means "Watch the cow."

Oriente incorporates the post-revolutionary provinces of Holguín, Granma, Santiago de Cuba, and Guantánamo, which are scenically and historically more interesting than most of central Cuba. The stunning landscapes vary from the north coast's exuberant banana and coconut groves clustered round thatched huts, little changed from Indian *bohíos,* to the towering peaks of the Sierra Maestra mountains and lush rainforest on the east coast. Some of Cuba's best beaches lie on the north coast of Oriente within sight of the mountains.

The wars of independence began in Oriente in the 1860s, and nearly a century later Castro concentrated his power base in the inaccessible Sierra Maestra. There are stirring monuments and museums recalling these periods in Santiago de Cuba, the latter dubbed "Hero City" for its many historic patriots.

The farther east you travel in Cuba the more Caribbean it feels. Santiago de Cuba is renowned for its contributions to Cuban musical culture; many of the greats of traditional sounds (Trío Matamoros, La Vieja Trova Santiaguera, and Eliades Ochoa, among others) all got their starts here. It continues to be the one place in Cuba where infectious music is inescapable.

Holguín Province

Holguín province begins bleakly around the busy capital but improves considerably as you travel north, where the countryside is lusher. **Guardalavaca,** 60 km (37 miles) from Holguín, is perhaps Cuba's prettiest resort, ringed by banana plantations and facing a gorgeous beach backed by a forest of sea-grape trees. Watersports are excellent here and at the equally picturesque—but isolated—beach of **Estero Ciego,** 2 km (1.2 miles) west. The resort's reputation is growing fast, and the Cuban government envisions it one day competing with Varadero. It is still in the early stages of development and, thankfully, extremely relaxed.

There are plenty of possibilities for excursions in the vicinity of Guardalavaca. To the west is **Bahía de Bariay,** which has a monument claiming Columbus's landing (a fact contested chiefly by Baracoa, farther east). Beyond the bay is **Gibara** (27 km/ 17 miles north of Holguín), a captivating if sleepy little port town.

The Guardalavaca countryside is truly a Cuban paradise—
the resort might very well be the prettiest on the island.

The national flag hangs proudly from the balcony of the Santiago city hall.

You can take a boat trip into the middle of Bahía de Naranjo to a simple aquarium, where you can swim with the dolphins.

About 6 km (4 miles) south of Guardalavaca, on a hill amid a forest of lofty palms and thatched homesteads, is **Chorro de Maíta,** the Caribbean's most important excavated Indian burial ground. Of the 61 skeletons on display, dating from 1490 to 1540 (more than 200 were disinterred), those in preconquest graves lie in a fetal position, while post-conquest skeletons lie in a Christian pose: outstretched with arms folded. Thick banana groves coat the hillsides along the scenic 30-km (19-mile) route south to **Banes,** a tumbledown town of clapboard houses with corrugated roofs. Fidel Castro was married at the church here in 1948, and the town's **Museo Indo-Cubano** has fascinating finds from Chorro de Maíta.

Santiago de Cuba

Many visitors prefer Cuba's second city (population 420,000) to the capital. **Santiago de Cuba** (880 km/546 miles southeast of Havana) is unpolished, has few grand palaces, and cannot compare with the colonial treasures found in Havana and Trinidad. But it is unfailingly vibrant and seductive, exuding a feel all its own. Enclosed by the Sierra Maestra mountains, Santiago can also be wickedly hot. *Santiagueros* negotiate their hilly streets by keeping to the shady sides, and they relax with little urgency on overhanging balconies.

Santiago is Cuba's melting pot, with a friendly population of predominantly mulatto people: descendants of Spanish, French from Haiti, Jamaicans, and huge numbers of African slaves. Afro-Cuban traditions remain strong, reflected in music (walk down any street and a cacophony of sounds emanates from unseen sources) and particularly in *carnaval,* now a pale shadow of its former self—due to lack of resources—but still Cuba's best.

Founded in 1514, Santiago was the island's capital until 1553. It is regarded as a "hero's city," and locals are proud of the city's rebellious past. Seminal events brought it center-stage again during the 1950s, when it assumed a major role in the revolutionary struggle. The attack on Batista's forces at the Moncada Barracks in 1953 thrust Fidel Castro into the national limelight, and it was in Santiago's main square that he first declared victory, on 1 January 1959.

An industrial city, Santiago was hit especially hard when Cuba lost its Soviet support and Eastern bloc trade partners during the Special Period. Perhaps for this reason, hustlers and prostitutes work overtime here to zero in on tourists' generosity.

Old Santiago

The most atmospheric part of the city is **Old Santiago.**
Castro delivered his victory speech in the heart of the old town, from the balcony of city hall on **Parque Céspedes.** More a plaza than a park, the attractive square is a genteel place with tall trees, gas lanterns, and iron benches. Old Santiago's grid of streets unfolds here, a few blocks inland from the heavily industrialized harbor. Parque Céspedes is dominated by its twin-towered cathedral. A basilica was

built on this spot in 1528, but what you see was rebuilt in the early 19th century after a series of earthquakes and fires.

On the west side of the plaza is the seriously handsome **Casa Diego Velázquez,** built in 1516 as the residence of the founder of Cuba's original seven *villas.* The oldest house in Cuba and considered one of the oldest in the Americas, it is in remarkable condition. Housing the **Museo Colonial,** its rooms overflow with fine period furniture and carved woodwork and encircle two lovely courtyards. Guides touch everything in the house, practically imploring you to sit on the furniture. Try to disregard the poorly realized reproductions of original wall murals around the courtyard.

Across the square is the elegant **Hotel Casa Granda,** which opened in 1914. Its terrace bar on the fifth floor affords excellent views of the cathedral towers and the city beyond.

East from the square, **Calle Heredia** is the epicenter of Santiago culture and tourism. The city's famous Casa de la Trova (music hall), which has hosted nearly all legendary Cuban musicians, is the centerpiece of both. Starting in midmorning, a succession of groups perform every style of Cuban music, from *son* and *guarachas* to *boleros* and *salsa.* Evenings in the intimate open-air space inside are the place to be. Calle Heredia is lined day and night with artisans and souvenir sellers.

Down the street is the **Museo del Carnaval,** a museum containing instruments, photos, and artifacts from Santiago's carnival. It also usually has Afro-Cuban music on weekends, as does the **Artex** store up the street. Also on Calle Heredia is the **Casa Natal de José María Heredia,** a cultural center and the birthplace of the Cuban poet who gave his name to this much-trafficked street.

Nearby, on Calle Pío Rosado, the **Museo Emilio Bacardí** has wide-ranging art, archaeological, and more recent historical collections (including a small, grotesque collection of mummies). The museum, in a shockingly grandiose neoclassic building on a beguiling little street, is named for its benefactor and the town's former mayor, whose family founded the Bacardí rum empire (which moved its headquarters and production to Puerto Rico after the revolution).

One of Santiago's most delightful people-watching spots is **Plaza Dolores,** a shady plaza lined with colonial-era homes (several of which are now curiously empty tourist restaurants). **Avenida José A. Saco** (more commonly called **Enramada**) is Santiago's main shopping thoroughfare, whose faded 1950s neon signs and ostentatious buildings recall more prosperous—and capitalist—times. Cobbled **Calle Bartolomé Masó** (also known as San Basilio), just behind Heredia and the cathedral, is a delightful street that leads to the picturesque Tivolí neighborhood.

In Tivolí you'll find the famous **Padre Pico** steps, named for a Santiaguero priest who aided the city's poor. Castro once roared fire and brimstone down on the Batista government here, but today you'll find more pacific chess and domino players who have set up all-hours tables on the steps. Take the steps up to the **Museo de la Lucha Clandestina,** the Museum of the Clandestine Struggle. This excellent museum, in one of the city's finest colonial houses, focuses on the activities of the resistance movement under local martyr Frank País. Residents of Santiago were

The Hotel Imperial is long gone, but its eye-catching 1950s sign remains.

instrumental in supporting the revolution, as were peasants in the Sierra Maestra. From the museum's balcony, there are tremendous views of Santiago and the bay (and, unfortunately, of plumes of pollution rising up from ill-placed industrial plants).

Not far from the museum is one of Santiago's best places to get sweaty in the evening. The **Casa de las Tradiciones,** a "cultural center" in a sweet little pink house (Calle General Lacret, 651), has live music and as much dancing as its tiny space will allow. It's great fun, and the locals usually outnumber the tourists.

Just west of the Padre Pico steps (south of the train station) is the one-room **César Escalante cigar factory,** unimpressive by comparison with other Cuban cigar factories but still an enjoyable place to visit, and the **Ron Caney rum factory.** The oldest rum distillery in the country, it was established in 1838 by Don Facundo Bacardí (whose descendants fled the country in 1959) and nationalized the following year. The rum produced here now goes under the name "Havana Club." You can visit only a small museum and bar.

Around Santiago

A good place to get your bearings on the suburbs of the city is from the rooftop bar of the lavish hotel Cubanacán Santiago, 3 km (almost 2 miles) east of the city's center. In the near distance you can make out the yellow **Moncada Barracks,** which Castro along with some 135 rebels attacked on 26 July 1953. The date is now a rallying cry and public holiday, and the barracks have been converted into a school and museum. The museum tells the story of the road to revolution using dozens of memorable photographs. Also on display are various bloodstained rebel uniforms, some of Fidel's personal effects from his time in the mountains, and "26 Julio" armbands (sporting the name of the resistance movement that developed after the Moncada attack). The bullet holes over the entrance are just for show.

North of Moncada, beyond the bus station, is the **Plaza de la Revolución,** a frighteningly polluted open square at the corner of Av. las Américas and Av. de los Libertadores. Massive spears thrust toward the sky in this monument to Antonio Maceo, a hero of the war of independence, who is seen riding triumphantly.

The fine **Cementerio Santa Ifigenia,** just north of the harbor (Av. Crombel and Reparto Juan Gómez), is the resting place of many Cuban heroes. Pride of place goes to the Cuban founding father José Martí, in a vast octagonal mausoleum designed so that the tomb catches the sun throughout the day. Look also for the tombs of Céspedes and Frank País; Frank's (as *santiagueros* refer to him) is marked like many others with the Cuban flag and the flag of the 26 July movement.

In an impressive setting 7 km (4 miles) from the city is the 17th century **El Morro Castle,** surveying the harbor mouth from a commanding clifftop position. Moated, thickly walled, and full of cannons, drawbridges, and passageways, it is in excellent condition. One room houses displays on pirates through the ages. A guide will point out a torture room with a trap door in the floor, through which uncooperative prisoners and slaves were reportedly dropped to the sea below. That's not a terribly appetizing thought, but the restaurant just beyond the castle, also called "El Morro," has gorgeous views of the sea and some of Santiago's finest food; it's a great place to get out of

Life Imitating Art

In Hemingway's *The Old Man and the Sea*, the fisherman pledges to make his pilgrimage to La Virgen de la Caridad should he reel in the big marlin. Hemingway, who scored the big one with his 1952 Nobel Prize for Literature, went to El Cobre and placed the award at the shrine. (It was later stolen, recovered, and permanently removed.)

Honor the patron saint of Cuba alongside the pilgrims that visit the Basílica.

the intense sun. The easiest way to get to El Morro is to hire a taxi, which costs about US$15 roundtrip (the driver will wait for up to a couple hours while you explore the castle and even eat lunch).

A place of great import (and considerable beauty) to all Cubans is the triple-domed **Basílica del Cobre,** named after the nearby copper mines that rise out of the forested foothills 18 km (11 miles) west of Santiago. Cuban faithful make annual pilgrimages to the church to pay tribute to its statue of a black virgin, the Virgen de la Caridad (Virgin of Charity). According to legend, Cuba's patron saint was rescued bobbing in the sea in the 17th century by three young fishermen about to capsize in a storm. With the wooden statue in their grasp, they miraculously made it to shore. Pilgrims, often making the last of the trek on their knees, pray to her image and place mementos and offerings of thanks for her miracles; among them are small boats and prayers for those who have tried to escape Cuba on rafts. The Virgen is on the second floor, encased in glass and cloaked in a glittering gold robe.

You can take a taxi to El Cobre for around US$15 roundtrip, although more adventurous sorts can hop a *máquina* (vintage American automobile taxi) or *colectivo* (bus or truck) out to the town and walk the mile or so to the church. If you'd like to stay overnight in this spectacular (and deathly peaceful) area, there is a *hostal,* **Hospedería de la Caridad,** behind the church, where foreigners who abide by the strict rules can stay for a mere five pesos a night (see page 133).

East of Santiago is **Parque Baconao,** a biosphere reserve spread over 40 km (25 miles). The local dark-sand beaches can be scrubby and the hotels themselves are isolated, but there's lots to explore in the park, and the Sierra de La Gran Piedra rise majestically above the coast.

A tortuous side road 12 km (7 miles) east along the coast ascends the mountains to **La Gran Piedra** (Big Stone), where you can climb on foot for a bird's-eye view of eastern Cuba. About 2 km (about a mile) beyond, a track leads to **Museo La Isabelica,** a 19th-century coffee-plantation *finca* (country house) with a workshop, original furniture, and a concrete garden where coffee beans were once laid out to dry.

> In Baconao park, visit Playa Daiquirí to say you sipped *"dye-kir-eez"* where Teddy Roosevelt and the Rough Riders landed during the Spanish-American war of 1898.

GUANTÁNAMO PROVINCE

You can reach Cuba's remote, mountainous, far-eastern region by continuing along the coast road from Parque Baconao; alternatively, you can backtrack to Santiago. The province has only one true tourist draw, but it's a super one: the magical little town of Baracoa. The only reason to stop over in the unappealing city of Guantánamo would be to visit the lookout point that is trained on the US naval base, an establishment that has recently been in the news for its role as detention and interrogation center for suspected Al Qaeda terrorists captured in Afghanistan.

The dry, cactus-strewn landscape of the south coast begins to change as you follow the winding, spectacular 30-km (18.8-mile) road "La Farola" across the mountains to **Baracoa** (150 km/93 miles from Santiago), a picturesque little village

Cubans and tourists flock to the Malecón in Baracoa— especially in early April.

known for its local chocolate and coconut factories. The tropical seaside town is surrounded by green hillsides covered with cocoa and coconut groves, and all around are palm-backed beaches and delightful, sinewy rivers. Named a UNESCO biosphere, Baracoa has no fewer than ten rivers. It's smack in the middle of the wettest region in Cuba, the reason adventure travelers have their scopes trained on the town's rivers, ripe for whitewater rafting.

That Baracoa was the first settlement to be established by Diego Velázquez in 1511 —making it the oldest colonial city in the Americas—is not in doubt. However, locals also claim that Columbus first landed at this spot (rather than near Gibara, north and west of here, as most historians believe). They insist that Columbus planted the Cruz de la Parra (Cross of the Vine) in the soil on his arrival. The cross is on display in **Nuestra Señora de la Asunción,** the church on Plaza Independencia. (Whatever the truth of the matter, carbon dating has established that the cross is more than 500 years old.)

Baracoa, though, has so much going for it that any associations with Columbus are a bonus. A good place to get your bearings is the hilltop **Hotel El Castillo,** a former castle looking out over old red-tiled roofs, the town's oyster-shaped bay, and the landmark mountain known as "*El Yunque*" ("The Anvil"), so named on account of its singular shape.

On Calle Antonio Maceo, you'll find people queuing for hot chocolate drinks in the baking tropical sun at Casa del Chocolate. Opposite is a charming Casa de la Trova, with rooftop performances. In the main square is a striking bust of Hatuey, the brave Indian leader who resisted early *conquistadores* until he was caught by the Spanish and burned at the stake. Also wander along the Malecón, the seaside avenue, from the snug **Fuerte Matachín** (an early 19th-century fort that has a small municipal museum attached) to the Hotel La Rusa, named after a legendary and glamorous Russian émigrée who over the years hosted celebrities from Che and Fidel to Errol Flynn.

In and around Baracoa are several dozen pre-Colombian archaeological sites related to the three major Indian groups that inhabited the town at one time or another. Only one native group, the Yateras, still exists.

Baracoa really shines the week of 1 April, when heady street parties every night commemorate the date General Antonio Maceo disembarked at nearby Playa Duaba in 1895, marking the beginning of Cuba's War of Independence.

"Gitmo"

Guantánamo, known to American military personnel as "Gitmo," is a curious anomaly in revolutionary Cuba. Where in the world is the US less likely to have a military base? Established in 1903 —making it the oldest overseas American naval base—the indefinitely leased land is a US reward from the Spanish-American War. The US stills sends its annual rent checks (about US$4,000), which haven't been cashed since 1959. To do so would be to recognize the legitimacy of the American presence in Cuba.

Cuba Highlights

Towns

Baracoa. A delightful small town, the first founded in Cuba, thick with tropical vegetation.

Havana. The island's capital: chaotic, but always enchanting.

Santiago de Cuba. The second-largest city, more laid-back than Havana, renowned for its historical importance and its music.

Trinidad. Cuba's storybook colonial gem, one of the finest in the Americas. Nearby are spectacular excursions to mountains and beaches.

Viñales town and valley. The scenic tobacco country is amazingly green; the somnolent town of Viñales is a charmer.

Experiences

Casas de la trova. Informal music halls, often lovely colonial buildings, where you'll hear the best Cuban music, from *son* to *guarachas* and *boleros*.

Dining at a *paladar*. You can also eat at a private restaurant, which might be in someone's garden, terrace, or even kitchen. Portions are huge and home-cooked, usually a great bargain.

Staying at a *casa particular*. As an alternative to a state-owned hotel, a private house is an invaluable opportunity (not to mention more economical option) to see how Cubans live.

Tobacco factories. Cuba's cigars are the finest in the world, and you can see them being hand-rolled up close.

Top Resorts

Cayo Coco and Cayo Guillermo. Isolated cays (keys) with a single large hotel on each. Excellent beaches and flocks of flamingos and migratory birds.

Guardalavaca. A lovely, relaxed beach in eastern Cuba with little development. Gorgeous, lush countryside all around; excellent excursions.

Playa Santa Lucía. A long stretch of perfect white sand in Camagüey province. Protected by an offshore coral reef; good diving and excursions to offshore cays.

Museums and Attractions

(Admission prices are in US dollars; note that in most museums, additional fees are charged for use of cameras and video cameras.)

Havana
Casa de la Obra Pía. Tues–Sat 10:30am–5:30pm, Sun 9:30am–12:30pm.
Casa Museo de Ernest Hemingway (Finca Vigía). Wed–Mon 10am–4pm.
Cementerio de Cristóbal Colón. Daily 9am–5pm.
Convento de Santa Clara. Mon–Sat 9am–3pm.
Iglesia y Convento de San Francisco de Assis. Daily 9am–7pm.
Museo de Arte Colonial. 9am–6:30pm daily.
Museo de la Ciudad de la Habana. Mon–Sat 9:30am–6:30pm.
Museo de la Revolución. Tues–Sun 10am–5pm.
Museo Napoleónico. Mon–Sat 10am–7pm.
Partagás Tobacco Factory. Tours Mon–Fri 10am and 2pm, Sat–Sun 10am only.

Beyond Havana
Jardín Botánico Soledad (Cienfuegos). Daily 8am–4pm.
Museo Farmacéutico (Matanzas). Mon–Sat 10am–5pm, Sun 9am–noon.
Museo Municipal de Historia (Trinidad). Mon–Sat 9am–6pm, Sun 9am–1pm.
Museo Nacional de la Lucha Contra Bandidos (Trinidad). Mon–Sat 9am–6pm, Sun 9am–1pm.

Santiago de Cuba
Basílica del Cobre. daily 9am–6pm; free.
Casa Diego Velázquez (Museo Colonial). Mon–Sat 9am–5pm, Sun 9am–1pm.
El Morro Castle. Tues–Sun 9am–6pm.
Museo de la Lucha Clandestina. Tues–Sun 9am–5pm.
Museo Emilio Bacardi. Mon–Sun 10am–8pm.

WHAT TO DO

ENTERTAINMENT

Although cultural activity has been under state control since the revolution and Havana no longer sizzles with the sleazy Mafia-funded casinos and clubs of the 1950s, both high culture and more down-to-earth nightlife thrive in Cuba. Outside the resorts, it can be hard to pin down what's going on where, but informal musical performances are ubiquitous. In the resorts, nightlife is focused around hotels, ranging from decent live bands, dance, and fashion shows to mimed Beatles sing-a-longs.

Live Music Performances

Cubans crave live music, and—with the surge in international popularity of traditional Cuban music—so do most visitors to Cuba. You certainly won't have to go out of your way to hear music performances. Roving groups of musicians can be found playing everywhere from airports to restaurants. Merely wandering the streets of Havana, Santiago, or Trinidad, you're likely to stumble across a party with a live band, or even a back alley where some impromptu jamming is going on. On Saturday nights in Camagüey, the music spreads to the streets in a "Noche Camagüeya" block party along Calle República.

All the styles of Cuba's delectable traditional music—*habaneras, son, boleros, guarachas, guajiras,* and more—can be heard in every town's *casa de la trova,* usually a fine old building on or near the main square. Performances are amateur and professional, take place afternoons and evenings, and are free or have a minimal cover charge (US$1–$2). Especially in the evenings and on weekends, when you'll encounter a vibrant mix of Cubans and foreigners, the island's *casas de la trova* really swing. The most famous is in Santiago de Cuba (which has sprung many a star), while those in towns like Trinidad, Baracoa, and Camagüey are especially charming.

Aside from traditional acoustic music, Cuba revels in salsa and jazz. Probably the best place for live jazz and salsa in the country is the rollicking Palacio de la Salsa, in Havana's slightly dated Hotel Riviera (Paseo y Malecón, in Vedado; Tel. 7/334501). There, from midnight on, Cuba's very best salsa bands perform (dancing is very much in order), and jazz artists entertain drinkers

Her name was Lola, she was a showgirl—the Tropicana is the premier Cuban cabaret!

in the adjacent bar from Thursday to Sunday from 9pm.

Other music hotspots include:

Havana. Casa de la Música (salsa; Avenida 35 and Calle 20, Miramar), Casa de la Trova (San Lázaro between Gervasio and Belascoán, Central Havana), and El Zorro y el Cuevo, (jazz; Calles 23 y O, Vedado).

Trinidad. Casa de la Trova (Hernández Echerrí, 29), Casa de la Música (Calle Márquez), La Canchánchara (Calle Villena, 70), and Casa Fisher (Calle Lino Pérez).

Santiago de Cuba. Casa de la Trova (Calle Heredia), Casa de las Tradiciones (Calle General Lacret).

Baracoa. Casa de la Trova (José Martí, 149) and Casa de la Cultura (Maceo, 122).

Cabaret

A legacy of the high-rolling casino days in Cuba, cabarets have been kept alive and well as an outlet for tourist dollars. Cavorting mulatta dancers in sparkling G-strings and pairs of strategically placed stars may not be most peoples' image of socialist doctrine—but this is Caribbean communism. While the best shows (at the Tropicana clubs in both Havana

A Musical Melting Pot

Salsa, rumba, mambo, cha-cha-chá, son, danzón—Cuba's rhythms are known the world over. Reflecting the mixed heritage of its people, Cuban music spontaneously combusted toward the end of the 1800s through the nexus of African and European cultures—in particular the love affair between the African drum and the Spanish guitar. In a typical Cuban band today you'll hear Latin stringed instruments in harmony with congas, timbales, and African bongos (all drums), claves (wooden sticks), and instruments made from hollow gourds such as the maracas and the güiro. Cuban percussionists are among the finest in the world.

First came son ("sound"), a style that originated in Oriente around the turn of the century. Son permeates all Cuban music and is the direct forebear of salsa; it has a percussive swing that is intrinsically Cuban. Mixed with jazz influences, it led to the brass-band salsa of famous groups such as Los Van Van, Isaac Delgado, and Irakere. Cha-cha-chá arrived in the 1950s, having developed from mambo, itself a blend of jazz and the sedate, European danzón of the ballroom. The rumba is typified by more celebratory, erotic dancing. Trovas (ballads) were sung in colonial times by troubadors in casas de la trova. After the revolution the trova evolved into the nueva trova, often with overtly political lyrics, made popular by such artists as Silvio Rodríguez and Pablo Milanés.

and Santiago de Cuba) are rather expensive by Cuban standards, seeing at least one big song-and-dance production in the flesh (so to speak) is de riguer.

The Tropicana in Havana (Calles 72 and 43, Marianao; Tel. 7/267-1717), founded in 1939 in a dazzling open-air arena, is indisputably the queen of cabarets. The likes of Nat King Cole performed here in pre-revolutionary times. With a 32-piece orchestra and a cast of over 200 (some parading in impossibly large headdresses), the sheer scale of the spectacle will make your head spin. The show regularly kicks off at 9:30pm, and a shorter performance follows later; there are also a restaurant and disco. Reservations and transportation can be arranged at your hotel for US$60. You can always visit independently, but the venue, situated in the suburb of Marianao, is tricky to find, and you might arrive only to find no tickets remaining. Havana's next-best cabaret show, smaller and less expensive, is Cabaret Parisien, at the Hotel Nacional (Calles 21 and O, Vedado; Tel. 7/333564), nightly at 10:30pm; admission is US$35.

The Tropicana in Santiago de Cuba (Autopista Nacional km 1.5, with signs from Plaza de la Revolución; Tel. 22/643036) fills an enormous, recently constructed complex on the city's northern outskirts. It is no less impressive than Havana's but a bit less gaudy. Admission is US$30, including a drink ($27 if purchased from a travel agency).

In Varadero, the Cabaret Continental at the Hotel Internacional (shows nightly from 8:30pm to 3am) pales in comparison with the former venues but is nonetheless an enjoyable and sometimes fairly raunchy song-and-dance extravaganza. A fun show—kind of Afro-Cuban with a pirate theme—followed by disco takes place in a cave at the Cueva del Pirata, some 9 km (6 miles) east of Varadero (Autopista Sur, km 11), nightly at 10:30pm until the wee hours. There is also a cabaret at the Meliá Varadero hotel.

Discos

Music is an integral part of Cuban culture—you'll never have to go far to find it.

Discos pulsate to both Latin and Euro-American rhythms. The places to be are Habana Café (the disco in Havana's Hotel Meliá Cohiba) and the disco in Santiago's eponymous hotel. These are glitzy affairs, where foreigners get soaked and approached by hustlers of all stripes. Also try El Galeón, in a make-believe pirate ship that sets sail from under Havana's La Cabaña fortress. The best in Varadero is La Bamba at the Hotel Tuxpan (entrance US$10–$15). Also try the open-air Discoteca La Patana, near the bridge into Varadero. In Trinidad, Motel Las Cuevas has a disco with live entertainment, but it pales in comparison to the music halls in town. In Guardalavaca, head for open-air La Roca, set just above the beach.

Bars and Cafés

Both bars and cafés are places to have a *mojito,* daiquiri, or shot of *ron* (rum), smoke a Cohiba, and—usually—hear some live Cuban rhythms. In Havana the bars not to miss are Hemingway haunts: La Bodeguita del Medio and El Floridita. Enjoyable café-bars in Havana include Café de Paris (Obispo and San Ignacio), Café O'Reilly (O'Reilly and San Ignacio), Montserrate (Avenida de Bélgica and Obrapía), and El Patio (Plaza de la Catedral). Several hotels also have good bars, including Hotel Sevilla (made famous in Graham Greene's *Our Man in Havana),* Hotel

Inglaterra's rooftop bar, and Hotel Havana Libre's Turquino (with amazing views from the 25th floor).

In Varadero, Bar Calle 13 (on Avenida Primera) is the place to meet the *jinetera* of your dreams. In Santiago de Cuba, the terrace bar on the 7th floor of the Hotel Casa Granda has splendid views and live music. A good place for a cold beer, paid in pesos, is Taberna Dolores, which usually has live music in its courtyard. At the corner of Calle Calvario is Café Isabelica, a venerable 24-hour bohemian haunt in a house three centuries old. It's the kind of place where tourists and Cubans seem to hook up in a matter of seconds. Baracoa's Hotel Castillo has a bar with sensational views and frequent live music.

The Classical Repertoire

The classical arts are greatly valued in Cuba, and drama, opera, classical recitals, and—above all—ballet can be enjoyed in theaters all around Cuba. Opulent, old-fashioned theaters such as those in Cienfuegos, Camagüey, and Matanzas, not to mention Havana's magnificent Gran Teatro, are sights in their own right. The best way to learn what's on is to visit the theater; performances are frequently limited to weekends.

The Gran Teatro in Havana, at Calles Prado and San Rafael (Tel. 7/613078), has two main concert halls and puts on a wide repertoire of entertainment, from opera recitals to ballet. It is home to the internationally renowned Ballet Nacional de Cuba; if you hear that the company (or the rather more innovative Ballet de Camagüey) is performing, be sure to snap up tickets. Havana's International Ballet Festival is held during the last week of October and first week of November.

In Santiago de Cuba, try to see the Ballet Folklórico Cutumba, a renowned troupe that delves into the world of Afro-Cuban spirituality and ritual. When in town, they perform at several theaters.

SHOPPING

Cuba has a reputation as a place where there's little worth buying. You will see incredibly barren peso shops—window displays with bottles of cooking oil, shoe polish, and a few plumbing parts. But there are plenty of things for dollar-wielding visitors to buy now that private enterprise is permitted on a limited scale. Tops on most people's lists are Cuba's greatest achievements (not including the national health care system): cigars, rum, and music. There is also an excellent selection of handicrafts available at excellent prices in towns and resorts frequented by tourists. Tourist markets are now thriving in Cuba's major centers, even if much of what you'll find is related to Che Guevara—berets, T-shirts bearing his countenance, and dolls, among many other "revolutionary" items.

> Like nearly everything else in Cuba, there is a black market for homes. Some foreigners have even skirted the complex laws and bought beach houses.

As for essentials, hotel and dollar shops carry mineral water, soap, shampoo, and toothpaste, but many medicinal or cosmetic staples are hard to come by; it's still best to bring all you need from home. Tiendas Panamericanas are well stocked dollar stores, but probably the most impressive dollar store in all Cuba is the Harris Bros. Company, a multi-story (it's got an escalator!) enterprise near the landmark Art Deco Bacardí building and the capitol.

Cuban cities are now an uneasy mix of sad peso stores and bright dollar shops, with an influx of goods most Cubans can only dream about (indeed, you'll see large crowds of people peering dreamily into shop windows). The uneven divide between communist ideals and materialist longings is one of the great contradictions in contemporary Cuba. Browsing along

shopping streets proves end-
lessly fascinating, though,
and provides profound in-
sights into Cuba's arcane
economy.

Souvenirs to Buy

Cigars and rum. The biggest
bargain in Cuba is probably a
coveted box of premium
cigars, which at home might
cost four times more. Cigar
factories open to tourists
have affiliated shops selling
all brands of cigars; the
Partagás factory in Havana
has a particularly good shop.
You can also purchase cigars

*Afro-Cuban handicrafts
make excellent gifts for
friends and family at home.*

at such Havana shops as Casa del Tabaco (Calle Obispo and
Bernaza) and La Casa del Habano (Calle Mercaderes, 120), at
hotels, and at the airport. You'll find Habanos shops in several
other towns and resorts (Trinidad's is on Lino Pérez, 296).

Bottles of rum also offer big savings. All tourist-oriented
and hotel shops sell rum, whether aged from three to six
years *(añejo)* or low-grade *aguardiente* (from sugarcane
alcohol) with humorous labels. Havana Club is the brand of
choice. Above El Floridita, Havana's Casa del Ron has the
island's most impressive selection of rums, including hun-
dred-dollar vintages, half a dozen national brands, and rum
flavored with grenadine, peppermint, or banana. The
dutyfree shop at the airport also has an extensive selection.

When buying cigars or rum, bear in mind the customs limits in your home country (see page 108).

Music recordings. Compact discs and cassettes of Cuban music are widely available, and the selection is now much improved. If you're in the market for Cuban recordings, look for CDs on the EGREM label, available in ARTEX stores (as well as others) across Cuba. Most are US$15 each. Recommended recordings include those by Trio Matamoros, Benny Moré, La Vieja Trova Santiaguero, Los Zafiros, El Cuarteto Patria, Los Van Van, and Pablo Milanés, just to name a very few of Cuba's excellent roster of popular musicians who will help you keep the fire burning back home. Musical instruments such as maracas, *clavés,* and bongos also make good presents.

Handicrafts. Local arts and crafts vary from tacky figurines to pleasant drawings of street scenes and postmodernist portraits. You'll also find evocative posters and black-and-white photos of Fidel, Che, and company. Fine handmade lace and crochet are available, principally in Trinidad. Those nostalgic for the old days might want to pick up a *guayabera,* the classic Cuban pleated, four-pocket shirt, worn untucked (occasionally you can even stumble across vintage linen versions). Boutique Quitrín (Obispo es. San Ignacio in Old Havana) has the nicest cotton versions of the original white *guayabera.* Much of the silver-plated jewelry is also a good buy, but you should refrain from acquiring anything with black coral—it's endangered and illegal to import in many countries.

There are more interesting things to buy in Old Havana than in the rest of Cuba put together. A lively open-air crafts market, with provocative art, Afro-Cuban and *santería* dolls, exotic woodcarvings, and hats made from stripped palm leaves, is staged daily east of the cathedral plaza, between Tacón and the canal. Plaza de Armas is busy with second-hand book vendors. Intriguing, hole-in-the-wall arts and crafts shops are concentrated along Calle Obispo. The excellent Palacio de la Artesanía (at Calle Cuba, 64 Peña Pobre y Cuarteles), in a 19th-century mansion, is a souvenir supermarket in a fine old mansion.

El Puro: The Cuban Cigar

Before launching the US trade embargo against Cuba, President Kennedy reportedly had an aide round up a supply of his favorite Cuban cigars. Now that cigars have again become chic, almost everyone knows that Cuban *puros* are reputed to be the world's finest. Factories produce more than 350 million cigars a year, with 100 million for export. Before the revolution there were more than 1,000 Cuban brands of cigars; today there are only about three dozen.

You can visit a number of cigar factories, where the rich aroma is overwhelming. *Torcedores* (the men and women who roll the cigars) wrap poorer-quality leaves inside better-quality ones with dexterous ease. Sacks of tobacco leaves are sorted into bundles, cigars undergo quality control tests, and prestigious labels are applied.

Buying a box of cigars can be daunting. People on the street will whisper "You want cigar, my friend?" and tell you that their sister (or mother or cousin) works in the factory and that the cigars are stolen. They may be hot, but they may also be inferior-quality fakes. (Cigars that cost US$375 in the factory or an official store might cost as little as US$20 or $30 on the street). Don't buy unless you know what you're doing. Proper-looking boxes are no assurance of authenticity; everything is counterfeited. In a shop, ask to look inside the box, take out a cigar, see if you like the aroma, and check for uniform color. The cigars should be slightly springy.

Handmade cigars vary in length from the 4.5-inch Demi Tasse to the 9.25-inch Gran Corona. As a rule, bigger cigars are of better quality and darker-colored cigars taste sweeter. Back home, keep your cigars moist: place them in a humidor or put the box in a plastic bag with a damp sponge.

Outside Havana, Trinidad has the best array of crafts shops in the country. Several streets just south of the Plaza Mayor (around the *casa de la trova),* known as La Candonga, stage a vibrant daily crafts market, and you'll find a good government-run crafts shops on Calle Simón Bolívar. Santiago de Cuba's crafts mecca is among the shops and vendors along Calle Heredia. The selection, though, is generally poorer than in Havana.

SPORTS

Watersports

Watersports enthusiasts are in luck in Cuba. Virtually every resort offers windsurfing, sailing, jet skis, and waterskiing. As anywhere in the world, motorized sports are expensive. Watersports centers are almost always affiliated with a particular hotel, but anyone may rent the equipment.

Diving is the area of greatest interest and growth. Cuba claims to be surrounded by one of the world's largest coral reefs, and more than 1,000 sunken wrecks. There are so many tropical fish

Art Buys and the Bureaucracy

If you purchase anything that can be described as art—even a cheap watercolor at a flea market—you'll need an official export permit to get it out of the country without hassle or fear of confiscation. A purchase receipt will usually not be sufficient. Most official galleries should be able to provide you with this. If the seller cannot provide you with documentation, you'll need to go to the National Registry of Cultural Goods, in the Vedado section of Havana (Calle 17, no. 1009 e 10 y 12). The permit costs US$10 and can take three days. If you haven't time for that, you can usually circumvent inspection by packing unframed drawings and paintings in a tube inside your checked baggage (angel fish, grouper, parrot fish, moray eels) and sponges that it can feel like swimming in an aquarium. Facilities are generally excellent, and prices are the lowest in the Caribbean. Nearly every resort has at least one professional diving center equipped with all the requisite equipment, from oxygen tanks to wetsuits. Most centers offer week-long diving courses for an internationally recognized qualification (such as CMAS or PADI) as well as two-day introductory courses.

Visitors can get certified in SCUBA at one of Cuba's many diving facilities.

Dozens of dive sites can be reached from resorts, typically a half-hour boat journey away. The diving center at El Colony Hotel on the Isla de la Juventud offers the best facilities and diving, but it isn't well suited to beginners. There are 54 designated sites, including caves, wrecks, and what is claimed to be the tallest coral column in the world. Resorts catering to all levels of ability include Playa Santa Lucía, María la Gorda, Cayo Largo, Varadero, Playa Girón (with good diving directly off the shore), Playa Ancón, Cayo Coco, and Guardalavaca.

Deep-sea fishing is one of Cuba's great attractions, though as of yet not well known (or over-fished). Trips leave from the island's resorts and Havana's Hemingway Marina in search of marlin, wahoo, and swordfish. Playas del Este, Varadero, and Cayo Largo are other places that offer excellent fishing expeditions. In addition, there are offshore expeditions for smaller fry such as tarpon, sea bass, and mackerel. For freshwater fishing, Hanabanilla and Zaza (near Sancti Spíritus) lakes both hold impressively big, copious largemouth bass. For information on fishing excursions, contact Puertosol, which operates the marinas in the main coastal centers (<www.puertosol.net>).

Spectator Sports

The national sport is baseball *(béisbol)*. Cuban teams are among the best in the world (and several stars have defected to the US major leagues). While children improvise with a stick and a makeshift ball in every town's open spaces, the main cities have vast stadiums. It can be difficult to find out exactly when a game is taking place; you should simply ask around.

ACTIVITIES FOR CHILDREN

At resorts, water-loving babies will be happy; those ages ten and up will be able to join in many of the activities. A few resort hotels (such as those at Cayo Coco) have children's clubs, and top hotels can arrange babysitting. Outside the resorts the facilities are limited, transportation can be problematic, and feeding fussy children might present diffi-

Kids... Little goats pull little folks on the streets of some smaller towns.

culties. But Cubans adore children and will certainly make a fuss over yours. Traveling with young families in Cuba can be a remarkable—and eye-opening—experience. If you travel with very young children, be sure to take all the diapers and baby food you require, as these items are hard to find in Cuba. If traveling by rental car, you should also supply your own car seat.

Calendar of Events

Reliable information about certain events might be hard to obtain. Contact the tourist board or a specialist travel agent before making plans.

January. *Carnaval* (Varadero). Lasts the whole month, with nightly street parties and processions once a week. Hotels feature Cuban dance lessons and competitions.

May. *Hemingway Marlin Fishing Tournament* (Hemingway Marina, Havana). Four-day competition begun in 1950 and won by Castro in 1960.

July. *Carnaval* (Santiago de Cuba). Cuba's most famous celebrations, featuring comparsas (street dances), are gradually being revived after cancellations between 1990 and 1993 because of economic constraints. The week-long event is focused around 26 July to tie in with the traditional end of the sugarcane harvest.

October–November. *Havana International Ballet Festival*. A gathering of top ballet companies from around the world, begun in 1960 and held alternate years.

December. *New Latin American Film Festival* (Havana). The most important film festival in the Spanish-speaking world, held during the first two weeks of the month. *International Jazz Festival* (Havana). A biennial, week-long festival with top jazz artists from Cuba and around the world: performances, workshops, lectures, and open rehearsals.

EATING OUT

It is a sad paradox that a land as fertile as Cuba should have such problems feeding its people. During the so-called Special Period of the early 1990s, food shortages became serious. Rations are still insufficient, with chicken, meat, and many other food items hard to come by. However, those with plenty of dollars (tourists and a small number of Cubans) are immune from hardships and get the most and best of what little is available.

Nevertheless, do not come to Cuba expecting memorable gastronomic experiences. Cuba once had a respectable *criollo* (Creole) cuisine, a fusion of Spanish and African culinary traditions. But many Cubans now have been reduced

> *¡Buen provecho!* — "Enjoy your meal!"

to eating simple box lunches and sandwiches; the tradition of sitting down to formal meals common in other Spanish-speaking countries seems all but lost here. Many restaurants have no choice but to offer standard airline-like "chicken or pork?" main courses, along with rice and beans (*moros y cristianos:* "Moors and Christians") and french fries. Most hotels play it safe by offering international fare.

Where to Eat

If you're based in a resort, you might face the potentially monotonous reality of eating almost all your meals at the hotel. Large hotels often have not only a main buffet restaurant but also a poolside *parrillada* (grill) and a beachside café.

State-run restaurants are of two types. Those for tourists offer food that is usually edible; you must pay in dollars. Those for Cubans have extremely limited menus and, generally, poor quality; waits are long, and pesos are the accepted currency. In some cities (like Santiago) it is possible to eat in peso estab-

Hotel buffets offer a wealth of sumptuous choices at an economical price — strictly turista fare.

lishments very cheaply, as long as you understand that perhaps only one item on the menu will be available and that Cuban diners might look at you as if to say, "How did you get in here?"

A third category is the *paladar,* a privately operated restaurant in a private home. These cater exclusively to tourists, who pay in dollars. For a while they operated clandestinely outside the law, but in 1995 the government legalized them. The maximum number of place settings is limited to 12. The food is consistently better than in state-owned restaurants, portions are larger, and the cost is generally more reasonable. Frequently you'll be offered a three-course meal, sometimes with a beer or juice included, for a set price (US$8–$12). You don't need any Spanish language skills to eat in a *paladar*— just an appetite and the bit of adventure that brought you to Cuba (and beyond the resorts) in the first place.

Official *paladars* pay hefty taxes to the state; unofficial ones operate on the sly, circumventing taxes but running huge risks by doing so. Whether or not it is a legal *paladar* has much to do with the ambience you can expect. Legal establishments are like simple, small restaurants, usually with menus, that just happen to be on the terrace or in a back room of someone's home.

In an illegal *paladar,* it is more likely that your hosts will merely make room for you at the dinner table. (Incidentally, it is illegal to serve lobster, which is meant to be offered in state restaurants only, but you will be offered lobster far and wide, at both legal and illegal *paladars.)* The tourist is under no obligation to establish whether a place is legal or not, and either one offers a valid, interesting Cuban experience—and probably a pretty decent meal as well.

In resort hotels and around Havana, cafés serve sandwiches (almost always ham and/or cheese), but otherwise snacks in Cuba are limited to bad street pizza and box lunches. Picnic food is an even more difficult proposition: hotel shops sell packs of biscuits and chips, while private farmers' markets sell fruit for pesos.

What to Eat

At large hotels, particularly in the resorts, breakfast can be the best meal of the day: a buffet featuring fresh fruit, fruit juices, cheeses, meats, and pancakes. Often there are also eggs made to order. In more modest hotels, sandwiches and omelets are generally the staple fare.

Hotel buffets are also offered at lunch and dinner, and guests with large appetites will find these a very good value. The food is "international" rather than typically Cuban. The surfeit of choices (several salads, piles of bananas, chunks of watermelon, cakes galore, a choice of fish, meat, and pasta) might make some travelers uncomfortable, given the ration books most Cubans must adhere to.

Most restaurants serve a Creole Cuban cuisine. Its main staple is rice and beans; you'll find either black beans or kidney beans *(congrí),* the latter typically served in the east of Cuba. Accompanying meat is often *pollo asado* (roast chicken) or *cerdo asado* (roast pork). White fish is commonly presented under the generic label *pescado* and is typically fresh and simply grilled; numerous restaurants also serve lobster at a hefty price (US$25–$30). Popular side dishes include root vegetables such as *malanga* and *yuca* (cassava) as well as *maduros* or *tostones* (fried plantains). Common desserts are *pasta de guayaba con queso* (cheese with guava paste) and delicious Coppelia ice cream, made all over the country.

What to Drink

The national drink is *ron* (rum), produced from cane juice and molasses, the by-products of the manufacture of sugar. Un-aged rum, called *aguardiente* ("firewater"), has a particularly high alcoholic content. Five- and seven-year-old rum, darkened and flavored in oak barrels, is drunk straight or on the rocks.

> *¡Salud!* — "To your health!"

Cuban cocktails make use of one- or three-year-old white rum. A number have achieved folkloric status: Hemingway drank his *mojitos* (sugar, lime juice, ice, fresh mint, rum, and soda water) in La Bodeguita del Medio and his daiquiris (sugar, lime juice, and rum blended into crushed ice) in El Floridita. Less exotic is the *Cuba libre:* simply rum and coke, often served with a slice of lime.

National brands of beer include Hatuey, Cristal, Mayabe, and Bucanero, all very drinkable (Hatuey particularly so). Only the most expensive restaurants serve wine, and the selection is usually limited to a few imported Spanish bottles.

ENJOY The BEST TROPICAL FRUITS
DISFRUTE de las MEJORES FRUTAS TROPICALE

| RUM COCO | RUN PONCHE / RON PONCHE | ORANGE JUICE / JUGO de NARANJA | SAOCO |
| | GRAPE FRUIT JUICE / JUGO de TORONJA | FRUIT COCKTAIL / COCTEL de FRUTAS | COCONUT / COCO |

Take your time with some of the sweet rum and fruit juice concoctions that you are sure to come across.

For soft drinks, try the wonderfully sweet *guarapo* (pure sugarcane juice pressed right before your eyes) or *granizado* (a flavored water-ice in a paper cone from ubiquitous streetside carts). In some towns, you may come across homemade cola stands, where they'll mix three shots of syrup with soda water (a good one is Trinidad's El Gallo Soda). It's amazingly refreshing and only about five cents.

Coffee is one of Cuba's main exports, but you don't always get export-quality coffee. A *café* is served espresso style and traditionally drunk with unimaginable quantities of sugar; *café américano* is weaker and served in a large cup. *Café con leche* is half espresso/half milk. Coffee with a little cream in Cuba is often disappointingly gray.

To Help You Order

Could we have a table?	*¿Puede darnos una mesa?*
May I see the menu, please?	*¿Puedo ver la carta, por favor?*
What do you recommend?	*¿Qué me aconseja?*
I'd like …	*Quisiera …*
I'm a vegetarian.	*Soy vegetariano.*

beer	*cerveza*	fish	*pescado*
milk	*leche*	soft drink	*refresco*
bread	*pan*	fruit	*fruta*
sandwich	*bocadito*	sugar	*azúcar*
butter	*mantequilla*	ice	*hielo*
salad	*ensalada*	tea	*té*
cocktail	*cóctel*	ice cream	*helado*
water	*agua mineral*	vegetable	*vegetales/ legumbres*
coffee	*café*	meat	*carne*
dessert	*postre*	menu	*carta/menú*
shellfish	*mariscos*	wine	*vino*

Reading a Menu

arroz blanco	white rice	*frito*	fried
langosta	lobster	*huevos*	eggs
asado	roast/grilled	*pollo*	chicken
naranja	orange	*jamón*	ham
bistec	steak	*queso*	cheese
papas	potatoes	*jugo de fruta*	fruit juice
camarones	shrimps/ prawns	*tortilla/ revoltillo*	omelette
papas fritas	french fries (chips)	*cerdo/puerco*	pork
		pan tostado	toast
congrí	rice and beans	*picadillo*	minced meat
frijoles	beans	*plátano*	plantain

HANDY TRAVEL TIPS

An A–Z Summary of Practical Information

A

ACCOMMODATIONS *(hotel; alojamiento; casa particular)*
Standards and facilities have improved dramatically over the past few years, thanks to heavy investment by Canadian, Spanish, and German companies in joint ventures with the Cuban government. Cuba's new or restored hotels in resorts and in Havana typically have swimming pools, restaurants, buffets, boutiques, air conditioning, and satellite TV. Resort hotels offer round-the-clock entertainment, from aerobics and Spanish classes to waterpolo matches and best-tan contests. Simpler resort hotels offer some in-house entertainment and invariably have a pool.

Elsewhere, hotels are much less enticing. Foreigners are billeted in large, Soviet-style concrete eyesores located on the outskirts of towns. Hot water is usually intermittent. Many smaller and inexpensive (peso) hotels do not admit foreigners.

Casas particulares—private accommodations in Cuban homes— are inexpensive alternatives that allow foreigners an uncommon view of local life. Be cautious when looking for a *casa.* The owners, or "guides" on commission, will probably find *you,* and a hustler's fee may be added to the cost of your room; it's better to avoid such intermediaries if possible. Visit the room before committing yourself.

Outside of such high periods as Christmas and New Year's, you don't really need advance reservations. It can be difficult getting through to phone numbers in Cuba; for reservations from abroad, a specialist agency in your own country might be of assistance.

I'd like a room ...	*Quisiera una habitación ...*
with twin beds/double bed	*con dos camas/cama matrimonial*
What's the price?	*¿Cuál es el precio?*
Is breakfast included?	*¿El desayuno está incluído?*
Is there a private homestay near here?	*¿Conoce una casa particular por aquí?*

AIRPORTS *(aeropuerto)* (see GETTING THERE)
Cuba's main airport is Havana's José Martí International Airport (Tel. 7/335777), located 20 km (12 miles) south of downtown Havana. Hotel

reservations can be made at the airport's Infotur office (see TOURIST INFORMATION). Varadero's Juan Gualberto Gómez Airport is 22 km (14 miles) west of Varadero. Santiago de Cuba's Antonio Maceo Airport is located 6 km (4 miles) south of that city. The airports in Camagüey, Cayo Coco, and Holguín are also international, handling charter flights.

On arrival, if you're on a package holiday a bus will transfer you to your hotel. Independent travelers can book transfers through specialist agencies in their own country; otherwise, take a taxi. From the airport, avoid expensive Turistaxis (white); yellow Panataxis are considerably cheaper (US$10–$12 to downtown Havana; $6–$7 to the center of Santiago). The trip takes about 40 minutes.

You must pay a departure tax (in dollars) at all airports: US$20.

B

BICYCLE RENTAL *(alquiler de bicicleta)*
With the scarcity of public transportation, millions of Cubans ride bicycles. Most resorts have bikes and mopeds to rent. Serious cyclists intending to tour the country should bring their bicycles, as well as plenty of parts and spare tubes.

BUDGETING FOR YOUR TRIP
Compared to the rest of Latin America and other developing countries, Cuba can be surprisingly expensive. Tourists pay for nearly everything in US dollars.

Transportation to Cuba. Unless you stay for a long time or in only top-flight hotels, airfare will be your greatest expenditure, especially if coming from Europe or Asia. Try to travel outside of high season (mid-December to mid-April) or on a package tour. Many find combination airfare-hotel deals cheaper than airfare alone.

Accommodations. Hotels in Havana, Santiago, and major resorts are expensive, comparable to North American and European costs. In resorts, all-inclusive deals (meals, drinks, and entertainment) can be a good deal. Private homestays in *casas particulares* are a quite inexpensive option.

Meals and drinks. Government-owned restaurants range from moderate to rather expensive. Lobster and other shellfish are the most expensive items. *Paladares* (private restaurants in Cuban homes) are an inexpensive alternative. Liquor and beer are slightly cheaper than in Europe.

Local transportation. Public transportation is cheap but woefully inefficient. Taxis and *bicitaxis* are the best way to get about within cities and resorts; they are inexpensive. Major expenditures will be excursions, whether organized group tours or independent trips made by bus or rented car (the latter is rather expensive). Dollar buses, trains, and even many domestic flights are relatively inexpensive.

Incidentals. Entertainment in cabarets and discos is expensive for Cuba (US$10–$60), and drinks in such nightspots are also much more expensive than in bars and cafés. Gifts like prestigious hand-rolled cigars are expensive, even if much cheaper than they are abroad.

C

CAMPING

Camping is becoming more popular in Cuba. There are two campsites geared to foreigners, with huts *(cabañas)* rather than tents. Aguas Claras is 7 km (4 miles) from Pinar del Río on the road to Viñales. El Abra is on the coast at Jibacoa, 40 km (25 miles) west of Matanzas. Both are inexpensive and attractive, with pool, bar, and restaurant. Contact Cubamar, the organization for camping (Calle 15, 752 esq. Paseo, Vedado; Tel. 7/305536).

CAR RENTAL *(alquiler de automóviles/ carros)* (see also DRIVING)

There are good reasons for not renting a car in Cuba. It's expensive, as is petrol (gasoline), and rental companies are inefficient and difficult to deal with in the event of car damage or other problems. If you wish to rent a car in one place and return it in another, you must pay the costs of having it returned to its origin (including the cost of a driver). However, public transport is generally poor, and while new tourist buses go to most places of interest, only a rental car will allow you to go anywhere and everywhere you wish, when you wish.

Cuba

To rent a car, you must be at least 21 years old and have had a year's driving experience. You will need to present a national or international driving license.

Cuba has none of the major international rental agencies found throughout the world. However, there are a good number of dependable local car hire firms with offices and rental centers at airports and throughout the island. Here are the main ones, with their Havana contact numbers: Cubacar (Tel. 7/332-277); Havanautos (Tel. 7/203-9658); Micar (Tel. 7/204-3457, 7/553-535); Panautos (Tel. 7/553-298); Transtur Rent a Car (Tel. 7/861-6788, 7/204-5532); Vía Rent a Car (Tel. 7/861-4465, 7/204-4445).

Rates range from US$45 to $80 per day for unlimited mileage. With limited mileage rates you pay an exorbitant 30 cents for every kilometer over 100 km (62 miles) per day. Insurance must be paid locally even if you have prepaid the car rental abroad. If there is any damage to the car, you must pay the first few hundred dollars worth of repair unless you can prove the accident wasn't your fault. You must leave a cash or open credit-card guarantee to cover for this eventuality. Inspect the car thoroughly before you set off to identify existing dents and scratches.

While the locals drive around in 1950s Cadillacs or 1980s Ladas, tourists are treated to fairly new cars such as Peugeots and Renaults. The least expensive models are not equipped with air conditioning.

I'd like to rent a car.	*Quisiera alquilar un automóvil/carro.*
for a day/a week	*por un día/una semana*
Fill it up.	*Llénelo, por favor.*

CLIMATE

Cuba has a subtropical climate: hot and humid. The chart below shows the average daily temperature in Havana. For beach lovers and sightseers, November to May is the ideal time to visit, though there is plenty of sunshine year-round. Hurricane season lasts until the end of November. The more active should avoid the height of summer, when it's debilitatingly hot and wet. As for regional variations, the mountains are cooler and the south and east drier and warmer. Oriente, the eastern part of Cuba around Santiago, can be wickedly hot—much hotter than the western region.

Temperature

°C	-30	-25	-20	-15	-10	-5	0	5	10	15	20	25	30	35	40	45
°F	-20	-10	0	10	20	30	40	50	60	70	80	90	100	110		

CLOTHING

Cubans dress very casually. During the day you'll rarely need more than shorts and a T-shirt (and swimsuit). In towns, wear walking shorts or long trousers. At night in winter, the temperature drops enough to warrant a light sweater or jacket. In upscale hotels, restaurants, and nightclubs, men are expected to wear a collared shirt and trousers and women are required to dress equally smartly.

COMPLAINTS

Package holidaymakers with a complaint should seek their company's local representative. If the complaint is serious, make a written and (where appropriate) photographic record, and deliver this to your tour operator when you return home. In addition to asking to see the manager *(jefe/gerente/director),* another course of action which often produces results is to ask for the complaints and suggestions *(quejas y sugerencias)* book.

CRIME AND SAFETY (see also EMERGENCIES and POLICE)

Despite the enormous disparity of wealth between foreigners and locals, Cuba is a remarkably safe place in which to travel—one of the safest anywhere. The crime that does exist is generally directed at possessions rather than people, so place temptation out of sight. Most top hotels provide safes, though usually with a rental charge.

City streets at night feel more dangerous than they actually are because they are so poorly lit. The one area where you should be wary of purse-snatchers is in Old Havana, particularly on Calle Obispo and the grid of streets south of it to the train station. Central Havana west of the Prado to the Hotel Deauville also has a bad reputation.

I want to report a theft.	*Quiero denunciar un robo.*
my wallet/handbag/passport	*mi cartera/bolso/pasaporte*

Cuba

my camera	*mi cámara*
safe (deposit box)	*caja fuerte*

CUSTOMS AND ENTRY REQUIREMENTS *(aduana)*

All visitors need a passport *(pasaporte)* that expires more than six months after your scheduled departure from Cuba.

Tourists also need a tourist card *(tarjeta de turista)* to visit Cuba. If you're traveling on a package holiday, the tour operator will arrange your tourist card for you. If traveling independently, contact your country's Cuban embassy; tourist cards (US$15) are also available from airline and travel agencies. The card is valid for 30 days. If you're planning to stay longer, the hotel at which you are staying can issue you a new card every month for a period of up to six months. Business travelers require an official business visa from the nearest Cuban consulate, which can take several week; a letter of invitation is usually required.

The US trade embargo does not permit American citizens to spend money in Cuba without special permission. There are general and specific licenses for government officials, representatives of international organizations, Cuban-Americans, religious or aid workers, researchers, athletes, and journalists. Those covered by a general license need no application or permission. Those wishing to travel officially with a specific license should seek permission from the Licensing Division, Office of Foreign Assets Control (1500 Pennsylvania Avenue NW, Washington, D.C. 20220; Tel. 202/622-2480) before contacting the Cuban Interests Section in Washington, D.C., for a visa.

Any US citizen who travels to Cuba without authorization by entering through a third country does so illegally. The Cuban government welcomes American visitors. In fact, Cuban immigration officials will not stamp American passports; they stamp only your tourist card instead. Fines are established at up to US$250,000, but no individual traveler has ever been prosecuted for entering Cuba without authorization. Upon your return you might be harassed and have Cuban purchases confiscated, but a "Don't ask, don't tell" policy seems to be in effect. Many opponents of the policy, however, freely choose to admit they've traveled to Cuba.

Restrictions for importation of goods into Cuba are: 200 cigarettes or 50 cigars or 250-g tobacco; 2 bottles of spirits. There is no restriction on the amount of dollars you can bring into the country, although officially you may not depart Cuba with more than US$5,000 in cash.

I have nothing to declare.   *No tengo nada que declarar.*

DRIVING

Road conditions. Driving through Cuba is largely blissful, as there is little traffic. Most main roads are paved and in good condition, although they are not always well signposted. The Autopista Nacional highway (motorway) runs from Havana west to Pinar del Río and east to Sancti Spíritus.

A number of rural roads are not paved. Beware of potholes: some are big enough to do real damage. Other hazards are columns of meandering cyclists and impromptu encounters with sheep, goats, and cows.

Rules and regulations. You must be 21 years of age to drive in Cuba and possess a valid driver's license. Drive on the right. National speed limits, strictly enforced, are 100 km/h (62 mph) on the highway (motorway), 90 km/h (56 mph) on other open roads, and 50 km/h (31 mph) in urban areas. You are likely to get an on-the-spot fine if caught breaking the speed limit. Wearing seatbelts is not mandatory, but insurance is. Most road signs are internationally understood. It's common practice to sound your horn when passing to let vehicles without rearview mirrors know what's happening.

Fuel *(gasolina).* Only gas stations owned by the state oil company, Cupet, may sell fuel to tourists. Though in past years travelers complained about being unable to find a gas station for miles once outside of major centers, this has mostly been rectified. Cupet stations are now spread throughout the country and are open 24 hours. Car rental companies might insist that you purchase expensive *"especial"* fuel, though pump attendants will supply the less expensive regular, paid for in dollars.

If you need help, contact Asistur: Tel. (7) 338527, (7) 625519, (7) 638284.

Cuba

Stop	*Pare*	Yield (Give way)	*Ceda el paso*
Caution	*Cuidado*	One-way	*Dirección única*
No parking	*No parqueo*	Danger	*Peligro*

car registration papers	*permiso de circulación*
driving license	*licencia de manejar*

How do I get to … ?	*¿Cómo se puede ir a … ?*
Are we on the right street for … ?	*¿Es ésta la calle que va a … ?*
Are we on the right highway (road) for … ?	*¿Es ésta la carretera hacia … ?*
May I park here?	*¿Se puede aparcar aquí?*
Full tank, please.	*Llénelo, por favor.*
I have a flat tire.	*Tengo una llanta desinflada.*
My car has broken down.	*Mi carro tiene problemas mecánicos.*

Fluid measures

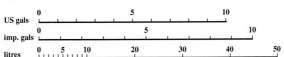

Distance

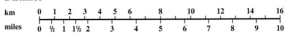

E

ELECTRICITY

Electrical appliances in hotels operate on either 110 volts or 220 volts. Some outlets accept flat-pin plugs, others round-pin plugs. Take an adapter; a converter might also be necessary.

What's the voltage?	*¿Cuál es el voltaje?*
adaptor/a battery	*un adaptador/una pila*

EMBASSIES

Canada. Calle 30, no. 518, e/ 5 y 7, Miramar, Havana; Tel. (7) 204-2516, (7) 204 2538.

United Kingdom. Calle 34, no. 702/4, e/ 7 y 17, Miramar, Havana; Tel. (7) 204 1771. The UK embassy also represents New Zealand interests and will help Australian and Irish citizens in an emergency.

United States. The US has an Interest Section (in Swiss embassy): Calzada e/ L y M, Vedado, Havana; Tel. (7) 333551. For travelers, this office acts in the same way as an American embassy.

EMERGENCIES (see also HEALTH AND MEDICAL CARE and POLICE) Asistur, a state-run organization, helps foreigners with medical or financial problems and is affiliated with a number of international travel insurance companies. For a 10 percent commission, they can negotiate a cash advance if provided with bank details overseas. They can also help with the retrieval of lost luggage and the issue of travel documents. Asistur's main office is at Paseo del Prado, 254, e/ Animas y Trocadero, Old Havana; Tel. (7) 338527, 625519, 638284. It has another office in Old Havana, at Calle Prado, 254; Tel. (7) 625519. Asistur also has offices in Varadero, Cienfuegos, and Santiago. All offices are open 24 hours.

Useful telephone numbers and phrases:

police	82-0116
fire brigade	82-0115
ambulance	40-5093

fire	*fuego*
Help!	*¡Socorro!*
Look out!	*¡Cuidado!*
Thief!	*!Ladrón!*

G

GAY AND LESBIAN TRAVELERS

Cuba is not as virulently anti-gay as are many parts of Roman Catholic Latin America. In fact, since the revolution Cuban society has become considerably more tolerant and inclusive. Still, discrimination and harassment exist, though they are unlikely to affect most gay travelers. *Jineteros* (hustlers) targeting gays are common. Areas known to be popular include the Malecón, the bars in Old Havana, and the bars and restaurants around the Coppelia ice cream park in Vedado. The Cuban film *Fresa y Chocolate* ("Strawberry and Chocolate") accurately depicts the frustration and discrimination still felt by many homosexuals in Cuba.

GETTING THERE (see also AIRPORTS)

Most flights into Cuba are charters. From Canada, regularly scheduled flights to Cuba leave from Montreal or Toronto, taking around four hours. There are also departures from Vancouver, Halifax, and Ottawa. Charters arrive at Havana, Varadero, and several other airports convenient to beach resorts. From the UK, scheduled flights fly from London and Manchester to Havana. There are also charter flights to Varadero, Holguín, and Camagüey (Playa Santa Lucía and Guadalavaca). From Australia and New Zealand, the options include traveling through Canada, Mexico, or other points in Latin America.

For those traveling legally to Cuba, regular flights to Havana from the US originate in Miami and (recently inaugurated) New York; soon to come are flights from Los Angeles. If you have authorization to travel to Cuba, contact Marazul Tours (Tel. 305/885-6161, 212/582-9570, or 800/223-5334).

Those wishing to circumvent travel restrictions from the US usually go through Canada (Toronto, Montreal, Vancouver), Mexico (Mexico City, Cancún), Bahamas (Nassau), or Jamaica (Kingston, Montego Bay). Branches of Havanatur handle tourist cards as well as roundtrip air tickets on Cubana Aviación. Their offices are in the Bahamas (Tel. 242/326-8643), in Toronto (Tel. 905/882-0136), in Montreal (Tel. 514/522-0358), and in Mexico City (Tel. 525/559-

3907). Similar arrangements can be made through Canadian, Jamaican, and Mexican airlines and travel agencies.

GUIDES AND TOURS

Most people still come to Cuba on package tours, which may include a group excursion or two. If you wish to travel independently and have found a hotel-airfare package that is cheaper than separate arrangements or airfare alone, note that you are not obligated to go along with the group once in Cuba. Plenty of people check into their resort hotels and take off on their own.

The most popular and straightforward way of exploring Cuba is on group excursions. However, these trips—available in any tourist hotel and led by carefully prepared English-speaking tour guides—may insulate you from many of the most interesting aspects of Cuban life. You can reach virtually the whole island from any resort on excursions; most are flexible and will allow you to break up a daytrip and stay overnight if you wish to explore on your own.

Freelance "guides," offering to take you to *casas particulares* and *paladares* (privately run lodgings or restaurants) or obtain cigars and prostitutes, are omnipresent in Cuba.

H

HEALTH AND MEDICAL CARE (see also EMERGENCIES)

Cuba's national health system has made it one of the healthiest countries in the developing world. There are no mandatory vaccinations required for travel to Cuba; nonetheless, some health professionals recommend vaccinations against typhoid and hepatitis A.

Although Cuban water is chlorinated and tap water is generally safe to drink, bottled mineral water *(agua mineral)* is widely available and recommended. The most likely source of food poisoning is from unhygienic hotel buffet food. Cuban food is very plain, and upset stomachs are less common than in many other countries.

The Cuban sun can burn fair-skinned people within minutes. Use plenty of sunscreen and wear a hat. It's also easy to become dehydrated, so be sure to drink plenty of water. Mosquitoes are a menace from dusk to dawn in coastal resorts. Air conditioning helps keep them at bay, but apply insect repellent.

If you need to see a doctor, contact your hotel's reception desk. Large resort hotels have their own doctor. All the island's main resorts have an international clinic *(clínica internacional),* as do Havana, Santiago de Cuba, Cienfuegos, and Trinidad. Medical treatment in Cuba is excellent and free for Cubans. Foreigners, however, must pay. Such treatment is expensive, so proper insurance is essential; make sure your health insurance has appropriate coverage.

Every town has an all-night pharmacy *(farmacia).* The range of medicines has become severely limited in recent years. Resorts have better-stocked international pharmacies, though prices can be astronomical. Bring all the medicines you might need during your stay, including mosquito repellent, vitamins, contraceptives, and insect-bite cream.

I'm sick.	*Estoy enfermo(a).*
Where's the nearest hospital?	*¿Dónde está el hospital más cercano?*
Call a doctor/dentist.	*Llame a un médico/dentista.*

HITCH-HIKING *(coger botella)*
Hitching a ride in Cuba is easy and safe. For millions of Cubans, hitching is part and parcel of everyday life. Great crowds gather on the outskirts of towns hoping for a lift. If you're driving a rental car, giving Cubans a lift is a great way to meet people and learn about their lives, provided you know some Spanish. If you're looking to hitch, the biggest problem you'll encounter is the paucity of vehicles (at least outside the major cities). As a visitor, you should always pay for the ride.

HOLIDAYS *(días festivos)*
The following days are public holidays in Cuba:

1 January	Anniversary of the Triumph of the Revolution: Liberation Day
1 May	International Workers' Day (Labor Day)

| 25–27 July | National Rebellion Day (26 July) |
| 10 October | commemorates the start of the War of Independence |

LANGUAGE

The official language is Spanish, but Cuban Spanish is spoken fast; consonants and whole endings of words might be swallowed. The language is more rhythmic and Caribbean-accented in Oriente.

You'll most likely need your high-school Spanish, especially outside tourist hotels and major resorts. Although young Cubans now learn English at school and elderly Cubans used English frequently before the revolution, few people speak English fluently.

Basic Phrases

Welcome	*Bienvenido*
Good morning	*Buenos días*
Good afternoon/evening	*Buenas tardes*
Good night	*Buenas noches*
See you later	*Hasta luego*
Please	*Por favor*
Thank you	*Gracias*
You're welcome	*Por nada*
Hello	*Hola*
Goodbye	*Adiós*
Do you speak English?	*¿Habla ingles?*
I don't understand.	*No entiendo.*
How much is it?	*¿Cuánto es?*

Days of the Week

| Sunday | *domingo* | Thursday | *jueves* |
| Monday | *lunes* | Friday | *viernes* |

Cuba

Tuesday	martes	Saturday	sábado
Wednesday	miércoles		

Numbers

1	uno (una)	16	dieciseis
2	dos	17	diecisiete
3	tres	18	dieciocho
4	cuatro	19	diecinueve
5	cinco	20	veinte
6	seis	30	treinta
7	siete	40	cuarenta
8	ocho	50	cincuenta
9	nueve	60	sesenta
10	diez	70	setenta
11	once	80	ochenta
12	doce	90	noventa
13	trece	100	cien(to)
14	catorce	500	quinientos
15	quince	1000	mil

The *Berlitz Latin-American Spanish Phrase Book and Dictionary* includes over 1,200 phrases useful for travelers.

MAPS

There are no detailed road maps of Cuba. The best maps (not on sale in Cuba and both slightly out of date) are Hildebrand's "Urlaubskarte Cuba" (1:1,100,000) and Freytag and Berndt's "Kuba/Cuba" (1:250,000); the latter is less up-to-date but has useful city plans. Of Cuba's metropolitan areas, only Havana and Santiago are too large to explore without a map. Hotels and bookshops in both cities sell reasonable maps.

MEDIA

You will not receive much outside news in Cuba, although many tourist hotels offer CNN. You might find a stray European newspaper at major hotels in Havana or resorts, but it's not likely. The main national newspaper, *Granma,* is the mouthpiece of the government. A weekly *Granma* international edition is published in English, French, and German, with cultural features of tourist appeal. Other national newspapers include the weekly *Trabajadores* ("Workers") and *Juventud Rebelde* ("Rebel Youth"). *Bohemia,* a respected monthly magazine founded in 1908, has in-depth analysis of contemporary Cuba and the world as seen through Cuban eyes.

Radio Taíno (1160 AM), a tourist-oriented music station with some broadcasts in English, is most easily heard around Havana. Tune in to the American Forces Network around Guantánamo on 102.1 FM and 103.1 FM for insights into life in the US naval base.

MONEY

Currency. As ironic as it might sound, the US dollar (*dólar* or *divisa,* the latter meaning "hard currency") is king in Cuba. The Cuban unit of currency is officially the peso, but in reality more and more goods are available only with dollars. Confusingly, prices in shops are displayed as $ for both currencies, though dollar prices may be marked "USD" to differentiate. The peso has no international value, and, as Cuba is desperate for hard currency, virtually everything tourists can buy (accommodation, food, drink, transport, souvenirs) is sold in dollars. Since dollar notes are in short supply, something called the "convertible peso" has recently been introduced. This is interchangeable with—and has the same value as—the dollar. Because convertible pesos have no value outside Cuba, you are allowed to exchange any you still hold at the end of your trip for dollars.

You may bring as many dollars as you wish into Cuba, but you would be wise to bring mostly denominations of $10 and $20, as it can be difficult to break $50 and $100 bills.

Currency exchange. There's little need to exchange currency unless you're determined to buy something in Cuban pesos. About all you can buy with them are stamps, fruit from markets, and perhaps a beer or rum in a local bar. *Casas particulares* and *paladares* require dollars. Even if a restaurant or bar accepts pesos, as a foreigner you will most likely have to pay in dollars. The official exchange rate is US $1=1 peso. Whether you exchange in an official *casa de cambio* (called a CADECA) or on the street, however, you'll receive 20–22 pesos for each dollar. The black market *(bolsa negra* or *mercado negro)* has essentially been eliminated.

Until 1993 it was illegal for Cubans to own or spend dollars, a policy abandoned in an attempt to bring into the official economy the millions of dollars swilling around the black-market economy. Now Cubans can spend their greenbacks in the rash of newly opened dollar-only shops in every town, and many Cuban-oriented restaurants and bars serving locals have started to charge in dollars, too.

Credit cards *(tarjetas de crédito).* American Express is not accepted anywhere, nor are any other credit cards issued in the United States; most Americans will thus need to fund their entire trip in cash. Most tourist shops, as well as upmarket hotels and restaurants, airlines, and car rental companies, in theory accept other major credit cards. (In practice, their willingness to do so might be another matter.) For large credit card payments, you will be asked to show your passport. Cuba remains a largely cash *(divisa)* economy.

Traveler's checks *(cheques de viajero).* Traveler's checks in dollars are accepted (in places that usually also accept credit cards), but they may not be American Express or others drawn on US banks. The easiest way to change traveler's checks into dollars is at hotels. Commission rates vary from 2 percent to 4 percent. Ask for notes in denominations of $20 or less, since few establishments can change $50 or $100 bills. If you've mistakenly arrived in Cuba with American Express traveler's checks, Asistur (see EMERGENCIES) can cash them for a 10 percent commission.

ATMs. Automatic cash machines are not yet a feature of Cuban life, although that is changing. A number of machines have been installed and activated in Havana. Your hotel in Havana (or Varadero, surely) will know if ATMs are in place by the time of your trip.

Do you accept traveler's checks?	*¿Cheques de viajero?*
May I pay with a credit card?	*¿Se puede pagar con tarjeta?*
How much is that?	*¿Cuánto es?*

OPEN HOURS
Offices are usually open weekdays from 8am to 5pm, with a one-hour lunch break. Some are open on Saturday mornings, from 8am until noon or 1pm. Banks are typically open weekdays from 8:30am to 3pm.

Some museums open daily, but most close for one day (usually, but not always, Monday) and also close on Sunday at noon or 1pm. Typical museum hours are 9am (sometimes 8am or 10am) until 5pm (sometimes 4pm or 6pm). Regardless of when you go, you'll find several closed for renovations; make inquiries before traveling a long way.

Restaurants do not typically stay open late; most close their doors around 9:30pm or even earlier. More modest restaurants often stop serving earlier, as they run out of food. The great exception is *paladares,* which are usually open from noon to midnight.

POLICE *(policía)*
Most Cuban police are helpful and friendly, even though they occasionally harass Cubans (or, specifically, anyone of dark skin color who might be assumed to be Cuban) accompanying foreigners. Some tourists find the ubiquitous presence of the police outside hotels and in the old town in Havana and Varadero disconcerting; others may find it reassuring.

Where's the police station? *¿Dónde está la comisaría de policía?*

POST OFFICES *(oficina de correos)*
You can buy stamps *(sellos)* with dollars at hotels, although this costs more than if you buy them with pesos at post offices. Cuba's post sys-

tem is extremely unreliable and slow. Postcards *(tarjetas postales)* sent to Europe take a month or more to arrive. Mail sent from abroad into Cuba often fails to reach its destination. Cubans typically ask foreigners to take mail home with them to post on their behalf to friends abroad.

Post offices are generally open weekdays 9am to 5pm and Saturday 9am to 3pm. You'll find post offices in every rural town; cities have several branches. In Havana, the best one to use is the one in the Hotel Havana Libre in Vedado (Calles L and 23).

More efficient mailing services are available through DHL Worldwide Express, with offices in several cities. In Havana, there's one in the Hotel Havana Libre.

PUBLIC TRANSPORTATION

With hundreds of people stuffed like sardines into buses and a return to horse-drawn vehicles, Cuba's public transport system is one of the clearest manifestations of the country's economic woes.

Taxis. There are several classes of taxis, which are your best option for travel within cities and resorts. State taxis are metered and fares are paid in dollars. White Turistaxis and Habanataxis are ubiquitous wherever tourists congregate; they are the nicest and, logically, the most expensive. Yellow taxis with blue markings are Panataxis, which are much more affordable; they can be hailed in front of major tourist hotels, at the airport, or summoned by telephone. Private taxis (which might or might not be licensed) also circulate. The lumbering vintage American automobiles with taxi signs *(colectivos* or *máquinas)* have fixed routes and are usually reserved for Cubans, though you might be able to negotiate a ride, paying in dollars while other passengers pay in pesos.

You can hire any taxi for a single fare or an entire day, and private taxis are available for overnight excursions (fee negotiated in dollars; do not expect bargains). A company called Gran Car rents swank vintage cars (with drivers) outfitted for tourist excursions: in Havana call 335647, and in Santiago call 686600. Many owners of private cars *(particulares)* also operate as freelance taxi drivers, even though it is illegal for them to pick up foreigners.

Buses (*guaguas,* pronounced "wah-wahs"). Buses provide the backbone of Cuba's public transport system, but they're not a great option within cities for tourists. There are too few of them, they're very uncomfortable, and they're usually impossibly full when they do arrive. The wait at bus stops has been somewhat alleviated by *camellos* ("camels"), flatbed trucks that can haul 300 people.

For travel between cities, towns, and resorts of major tourist interest, however, there is a new type of *guagua.* A company named Víazul (Av. 26 e/ Av. Zoológico y Ulloa, Vedado; Tel. 811413, 811108, 815652) operates air-conditioned and very comfortable tour buses to Varadero, Viñales/Pinar del Río, Cienfuegos, Trinidad, Santa Clara, Sancti Spíritus, Ciego de Ávila, Camagüey, Holguín, Las Tunas, Bayamo, and Santiago de Cuba. Prices range from $10 (Havana to Varadero) to $51 (Havana to Santiago), with payment in dollars. If you're not renting an automobile in Cuba but traveling independently, Víazul is the way to go. It's far more efficient, faster, and more reliable (if slightly more expensive) than trains.

Trains (*trenes*). Cuba was the first country in Latin America to have a railroad system, but things haven't improved much since then. Trains can be a real adventure in Cuba, but you'd best be prepared for it. Journeys are extremely slow (16 hours from Havana to Santiago), schedules are unreliable, and breakdowns and stoppages on the tracks are frequent (that 16-hour journey can turn into 22). Trains usually run only on alternate days or a couple of times a week to most destinations. That said, stations and trains themselves are wonderfully atmospheric. Those who pay in dollars can travel in relative comfort and make bookings through Ladis offices located at train stations (Havana: Tel. 7/621770; Santiago: Tel. 22/622254). You're advised to make reservations well in advance for most trips.

Domestic flights. Flying in Cuba is the quickest and most reliable form of transport for long trips. It's also good value (flights range from about $25 to $85 each way). Flights fill up fast, so book in advance from your home country if possible. Cubana, the national airline, provides most domestic flights, including those from Havana to Baracoa, Camagüey, Cayo Largo, Ciego de Ávila, Cienfuegos, Guantánamo,

Cuba

Holguín, Nueva Gerona (Isla de la Juventud), Santiago, and Varadero. Frequency varies enormously, from several daily flights to Santiago to twice weekly to Baracoa. Tickets can be purchased in Cubana offices around the country or from the main office in Havana on Calle 23 (La Rampa), no. 64, e/ P y Infanta (Tel. 7/334949).

Bicycle taxis. *Bicitaxis,* Cuba's pedicabs, are just as plentiful as automobile taxis and a fun way to traverse the city on short trips. Fares are paid in dollars; most trips end up costing about as much as a Panataxi ($2–$4). But you'll see more of the city—and, of course, breathe more fumes, since you sit in an open carriage behind the driver.

Horse carts *(coches).* Due to fuel shortages, in virtually every city except Havana and Santiago there are horses pulling carts and plush little carriages up and down the main streets. Ironically, horse carriages acting as taxis have become a tourist attraction in the resorts.

When's the next bus/train to…?	*¿Cuándo sale el próximo autobús/tren para…?*
bus station	*estación de autobuses*
What's the fare to…?	*¿Cuánto es la tarifa a…?*
A ticket to…	*Un billete para…*
single (one-way)	*ida*
return (roundtrip)	*ida y vuelta*

 R

RELIGION

Roman Catholicism in Cuba is strongly rivaled by syncretic Afro-Cuban religions such as *santería* (see page 26). Many aspects of these religious practices can be experienced by visitors. The communist government blunted the power and influence of the Catholic Church in the early 1960s (for example, by abolishing religious holidays). Mass, however, is still said in numerous churches throughout the island, and since the Pope's visit to Cuba in 1998 there has been a resurgence of Catholic practice—and a seeming relaxation of hostility from the government.

T

TELEPHONE *(teléfono)*

Cuba's country code is 53. In addition, each area of the island has its own area code; for Havana it is 7.

To make an international call from your hotel room, dial 8 or 88 before the country code; on card phones dial 119. To make a domestic call, add the area code (for example, 7 for Havana).

Top hotels have direct-dial facilities for all calls. Elsewhere you can make domestic calls on a direct line, but you will need to go through the hotel operator for international calls. With upgrading, telephone numbers are constantly changing; several of the phone numbers listed in this guide may have changed.

The easiest and least expensive place to make domestic and international calls is from ETECSA phone booths: glass boxes with banks of phones that take phone cards, which they also sell (in denominations of $10 and $20). More and more card phones are available throughout Cuba. Instructions in Spanish should be posted by the phone.

International calls from Cuba are very expensive (from $3–$6 per minute). As they do everywhere in the world, hotels charge a significant surcharge on calls. From a private telephone, you can make only reverse-charge (collect) calls, a possibility in *casas particulares*.

I'd like make a telephone call ...	*Quisiera hacer una llamada ...*
to England/Canada/United States.	*a Inglaterra/Canadá/ Estados Unidos.*
reverse-charge call	*cobro revertido*
Can you get me this number in ... ?	*¿Puede comunicarme con este número en ... ?*
phone card	*tarjeta telefónica*

TIME ZONES

Cuba is five hours behind GMT. It operates on Eastern Standard Time in winter and Daylight Savings Time (one hour later) from April to October.

Cuba

San Francisco	Cuba	New York	London	Sydney
9am	noon	noon	5pm	3am

TIPPING *(propina)*

In restaurants and *paladares,* tip $1 to $2 per person, or 10 percent (always in dollars). In bars, loose (American) change is acceptable. Tour guides expect at least a couple of dollars for their services, and roving musical groups should be given a dollar. In almost any other situation, a dollar is a very generous tip, and loose change might be more appropriate.

TOILETS *(baños/servicios)*

It's often best to carry a roll of toilet paper with you at all times in Cuba, as many establishments do not always provide their own.

TOURIST INFORMATION

There are official Cuban government tourism offices in Canada and Britain but not in the United States:

Canada. Cuba Tourist Offices in Montréal (440 Blvd. René Levesque, Suite 1402, Montréal, Quebec H2Z 1V7; Tel. 514/875-8004) and Toronto (55 Queen St. East, Suite 705, Toronto, Ontario M5C 1R6; Tel. 416/362-0700).

UK. Cuba Tourist Board, 167 High Holborn, London WC1V 6PA; Tel. (020) 7240 6655.

In Cuba itself, there is no centralized system providing tourism information, and reliable information is sometimes hard to come by. Instead, you must rely upon hotels and travel agencies, whose primary function is to sell excursion packages. In Cuba all hotels have a tourism desk *(buró de turismo).*

For queries about the city of Havana, you'll find Infotur offices at the airport, on the Parque Central by the Hotel Plaza, and in Old Havana at Calle Obispo 358 (<www.infotur.cu>). In Varadero, information can be obtained from Havanatur, Ave. Playa 3606, e/Calle 36 y Calle 37 (Tel. 5/663713, <www.havanatur.cu>). These and other state travel agencies (Cubatur, Cubanacán) handle excursions, transfers, and other arrangements on behalf of foreign tour operators.

Other agencies selling excursions (but also providing tourist information on-site) are Rumbos and Tour and Travel (Tel. 7/554082).

If you need a particular address or phone number, ask to see the *Directorio Turístico de Cuba* (Cuban Tourist Directory).

WEBSITES

Because few Cubans have access to the Internet, Cuba is surprisingly well served by the Web. From sites about the US embargo and travel restrictions to traveler recommendations, there is a wealth of information about Cuba on the World Wide Web. Your favorite browser will turn up many sites when you search the words Cuba travel.

A few sites worth exploring include the following:

<www.dtcuba.com> (Cuban Tourist Directory site)
<www.cubaweb.cu> (official government site)
<www.cubalinda.com>
<www.cubatravel.cu>
<www.infotur.cu>. Information in Havana.
<www.havananatur.cu>. Information in Varadero and elsewhere.
<www.usacubatravel.com>. Information for travelers from the US.

WEIGHTS AND MEASURES

Cuba uses the metric system: meters, kilometers, liters, and kilograms.

Length

Weight

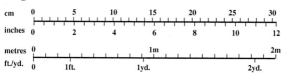

Recommended Hotels

The very best hotels are joint ventures with private firms from Spain, Canada, and other countries. These are of an international standard. Many others, though (even some of those with four stars), are a notch or two down from what you'd expect in Europe, North America, or Asia. At the inexpensive level, hotels are usually quite lacking in ambience and amenities.

Casas particulares—accommodations in private homes—are not only a better-quality and much cheaper alternative to the inexpensive hotels; they allow you a glimpse into unguarded Cuban life. In general, a house will have from one to three rooms available, with an occasional apartment. They generally cost $15–$30 per room. Your hosts might also offer breakfast and home-cooked meals.

You'll find a very abbreviated list of recommended private-home *casas* following the regular hotel listings below; however, others are very easy to find. In general, it is not permissible to bring "guests" (i.e., Cuban "dates") to your room. (See ACCOMMODATIONS, page 103.)

The price categories below, in US dollars, are for a standard double room, excluding meals, in high season (mid-December to mid-April, July to August). Prices drop by 15–30 percent during other months. If you're not traveling on a package tour, prepare to pay with dollars (in cash or with traveler's checks). Only top hotels accept credit cards; remember that credit cards issued by American Express or drawn on US banks are not accepted in Cuba.

Reservations are most necessary in Havana and the major resorts. Faxing hotels for reservations from abroad is not very practical, as many cannot return international faxes. It is best to call directly and get a confirmation number or name of the person you spoke with. Cuba's country code is 53.

$$$$	over $150
$$$	$100–$150
$$	$50–$100
$	under $50

HAVANA

Old Havana

Ambos Mundos $$$ *Obispo esq. Mercaderes, Habana Vieja; Tel. (7) 866-9530; fax (7) 866-9532, <www.hotelambosmundo. com>.* Hemingway wrote much of *For Whom the Bell Tolls* in room 511 of this historic hotel (opened in 1920). It's in the heart of Old Havana, on one of its most picturesque streets. The hotel was gloriously restored in 1997, and rooms are nicely decorated. On the ground floor is an airy, lovely piano bar. 50 rooms.

Hostal Valencia $$ *Officios, 53 esq. Obrapía, Habana Vieja; Tel. (7) 862-3801; fax (7) 833-5628.* In an 18th-century mansion between Plaza de Armas and Plaza Vieja, this small Spanish-style yellow colonial is utterly charming. One of the city's best deals, it features rooms surrounding a delightful green court-yard. Fine Spanish restaurant. Book well in advance. 12 rooms.

Hotel Sevilla $$$$ *Trocadero, 55 e/ Zulueta y Prado, Habana Vieja; Tel. (7) 860-8560; fax (07) 860-8582.* This recently restored turn-of-the-century establishment, a classic of Spanish and Moroccan inspiration, is again one of the best in the old city. It has a sumptuous lobby, magnificent rooftop restaurant, and other excellent dining options. Guests have included Al Capone, Josephine Baker, and Enrico Caruso, and scenes from Greene's *Our Man in Havana* were set here. Rooms are comfortable and stylish. Good pool, gymnasium. 179 rooms.

Hotel Santa Isabel $$$$ *Calle Baratillo, 9 e/ Obispo y Narciso López, Habana Vieja; Tel. (7) 833-8201; fax (7) 833-8391; <www.hotelsantaisabel.cu>.* Havana's most magnificent and posh place to stay is this small, quiet, gorgeously restored hotel. It's in an 18th-century palace right on the Plaza de Armas, the city's oldest. Sumptuous rooms have period furniture, and the hotel features a lovely courtyard and great views from the roof. Prices include breakfast. 27 rooms.

Hotel Florida $$$ *Calle Obispo esq. Cuba, Habana Vieja; Tel. (7) 862-4127; fax (7) 862-4117, <www.hotelflorida.cu>.* Havana's newest hotel, in a marvelous colonial mansion built in 1836, achieves affordable luxury. It originally became a hotel in 1885 but reopened only in 1999. It is extremely elegant, with plush public rooms, a lovely courtyard, and a great location just a couple of blocks from the Plaza de Armas. Some rooms have balconies. Piano bar, lobby bar, and restaurant. 25 rooms.

Residencia Académica Convento de Santa Clara $-$$ *Calle Cuba, 610 e/ Luz y Sol, Habana Vieja; Tel. (7) 861-3335; fax (7) 833-5696.* One of the more unusual places to stay is this quiet, sunny former convent, a section of which has been converted into a simple hotel. Rooms are plain; many guests are here for long-term stays. The hotel's multi-room suite is one of the best bargains you will find in the area. Prices include breakfast. 9 rooms.

New Havana

Meliá Cohiba $$$$ *Paseo e/ 1 y 3, Vedado; Tel. (7) 833-3636; fax (7) 833-4555.* Cuba's most expensive place to stay has all the trappings of a large, top-flight international hotel. Its location in western Vedado may not be ideal for tourists who'll be spending most of their time in Old Havana. The hotel has a popular bar-disco, Habana Café, and a cigar bar. Prices include breakfast. 462 rooms.

Hotel Nacional \$\$\$\$ *Calle O esq. 21, Vedado; Tel. (7) 873-3564; fax (7) 873-3899, <www.hotelnacionaldecuba.com>*. A classic feature of New Havana, this landmark 1930 hotel rises above the Malecón. Rooms are large, and most have sea views. Wormold was nearly poisoned here in *Our Man in Havana,* but the cuisine is considerably better now. It has a stunning dining room, two pools, a nightly cabaret show, gardens, terraces, and stylish bars. Prices include breakfast. 467 rooms.

PINAR DEL RÍO PROVINCE

La Ermita \$–\$\$ *Carretera de la Ermita, km 2, Viñales; Tel. (8) 936071; fax (8) 936069.* Rooms around the pool at this contemporary, low-slung hotel of Spanish colonial design have some of the finest views in the country. The verdant valley and spectacular sunsets fill the horizon. Rooms are standard, but most have balconies (ask for one facing the valley). An enjoyable 20-minute walk from Viñales town. Excellent value. 62 rooms.

Los Jazmines \$\$ *Carretera de Viñales, km 25 (2 km from Viñales); Tel. (8) 936205; fax (8) 936215.* This pretty-in-pink hotel on the edge of the beautiful Viñales valley has stupendous panoramic views. Fetching bedrooms with balconies, excellent pool; horseback riding available. Excellent value. 48 rooms.

Isla de la Juventud

El Colony \$\$ *Carretera de Sigueanea, km 16; Tel. (46) 398181, fax (46) 398420.* On the coast, 42 km (26 miles) southwest of Nueva Gerona, this is an isolated, overpriced 1950s tourist enclave of exclusive interest to divers. The hotel itself and its beach are unappealing. Lots of activities. 77 rooms.

Cuba

Villa $$ *Autopista Nueva Gerona, La Fé, km 1; Tel. (46) 323290; fax: (46) 324486.* Modest but well-maintained riverside complex set around a decent pool, just outside Nueva Gerona. Rooms are spacious, modern. Many activities, including disco and aerobics. 23 rooms.

Cayo Largo

Isla del Sur $$$ (also **Villa Capricho, Villa Iguana, Villa Coral**) *Tel. (45) 48111; fax (45) 48201.* Four adjacent beachside complexes share comprehensive leisure facilities. The most romantic is Villa Capricho, with vaulted, thatched bungalows set amid palms on the beach. Villa Coral, with small villas around an enticing pool, is the most stylish. 60–72 rooms at each hotel.

MATANZAS PROVINCE

Varadero

Cuatro Palmas $$–$$$ *Avenida 1ra e/ 61 y 62; Tel. (45) 667040; fax (45) 667208.* An attractive beachside complex of colonial-style villas and bungalows situated right in the center of the resort. Some of the rooms (which can be a little worn) are arranged around an excellent pool. 340 rooms.

Varadero Internacional $$ *Av. Las Américas; Tel. (45) 667038; fax (45) 667246.* Varadero's renowned 1950s hotel has plenty of style: its buffet dinners and Cabaret Continental are the best in town. Huge range of facilities. Rooms are a bit dated, divided between bungalows in gardens and large rooms overlooking the good stretch of beach. 371 rooms.

Meliá Las Américas $$$–$$$$ *Carretera Las Morlas, Playa Las Américas; Tel. (45) 667600; fax (45) 667625.* This swank, Spanish-run, five-star hotel matches its Meliá neighbor for quality and facilities. Las Américas is newer, smaller, and more demure. 250 rooms.

Meliá Varadero $$$$ *Autopista del Sur, Playa Las Américas; Tel. (45) 667013; fax (45) 667012.* A dazzling mega-complex at the resort's far eastern end with tons of amenities: high-rise atrium, fountain, vast pool, three restaurants, disco, shops, and more. Rooms have sofas, and most have good views. Direct beach access. 490 rooms.

Zapata Peninsula

Villa Guamá $ *Laguna del Tesoro, Ciénaga de Zapata; Tel. (59) 2979.* Reached by boat, this is one of the most distinctive places to stay in Cuba. Thatched huts are spread over a series of interconnected islands in the middle of a swamp. Mosquito repellent essential. 59 rooms.

CENTRAL CUBA

Cienfuegos

Jagua $$ *Calle 37, no. 1, Punta Gorda; Tel. (432) 551003; fax (432) 551245.* An ugly 1950s building and former casino hotel in a good position on the edge of the bay, with reasonable facilities, including a nightly cabaret. 145 rooms.

Trinidad

Hotel Ancón $$ *Playa Ancón; Tel. (419) 6120; fax (419) 6122.* Isolated on the excellent beach 16 km (10 miles) from Trinidad, a modern but uninspiring block perched on white sands with sea views. Comprehensive watersports facilities. All-inclusive meal plans available. 279 rooms.

Cuba

Hotel Las Cuevas $$ *Finca Santa Ana; Tel. (419) 6133; fax (419) 6161.* On a hill overlooking the town, this peculiar place is Trinidad's only decent hotel, a 20-minute walk from the center of old town. Small concrete block cabañas spread out across a hillside, with an acceptable pool and disco. 124 rooms.

Cayo Coco

Tryp Cayo Coco $$$ *Cayo Coco; Tel. (33) 301300; fax (33) 301375.* Cuba's most attractive resort hotel, a replica of a colonial village amid palmy gardens and alongside a dazzling white, 4-km beach. Pastel-colored villas interwoven by a magnificent sculpted pool. Excellent staff, watersports, six restaurants, shops. 966 rooms.

Camagüey

Gran Hotel $–$$ *Calle Maceo, 67; Tel. (32) 292093, fax (32) 293933.* This colonial building in the heart of Camagüey has been a hotel since 1937. Handsome, old-style lobby and nice suites. Most rooms have balconies. 72 rooms.

Playa Santa Lucía

Hotel Caracol $$–$$$ *Playa Santa Lucía; Tel. (32) 30403; fax (32) 335043.* The resort's prettiest hotel has floral gardens and modern villas with fancy bedrooms, each with balcony and sitting area. Full range of activities and facilities. 150 rooms.

ORIENTE: THE EAST

Guardalavaca

Las Brisas $$$ *Playa Guardalavaca; Tel. (24) 30218; fax (24) 30418.* This all-inclusive Canadian venture offers a choice of candlelit restaurants, an attractive pool, direct beach access, full range of watersports and activities, in-house entertainment. 230 rooms.

Santiago de Cuba

Meliá Santiago de Cuba $$$–$$$$ *Av. de las Américas y Calle M; Tel. (22) 687070; fax (22) 687170.* A postmodernist, multicolored tower block, this is Cuba's most ostentatious hotel. Six bars (one with spectacular views from the rooftop), a luxurious pool, indulgent buffets, snazzy nightclub, obsequious staff. At 3 km (2 miles) from the city center, it's inconvenient but big enough to handle groups. 308 rooms.

Hotel Casa Granda $$$ *Heredia, 201 (on Parque Céspedes); Tel. (22) 686600; fax (22) 686035.* A grand white building in the heart of Santiago, overlooking the main plaza, this classic hotel has been recently renovated and restored to its former status. In its heyday Joe Louis and Graham Greene's "Man in Havana" stayed here. By far the best place to stay in the city; ask for a plaza view. Terrace bar with great views (non-guests admitted for $2, including a drink). Prices include breakfast. 55 rooms.

Villa $–$$ *Av. Manduley, 502 e/ 19 y 21, Vista Alegre; Tel. (22) 641368, fax (22) 687166.* Four km (2.5 miles) from the city center in a peaceful suburb, this hotel has a secluded pool and good accommodations (especially superior rooms) scattered among old villas. 50 rooms.

Hospedería de la Caridad $ *behind Basílica del Cobre, El Cobre; Tel. (22) 36246.* Simple, convent-like accommodations for those making pilgrimages to the Virgin de la Caridad—and those who want an alternative, serene, dirt-cheap experience. 13 rooms.

Parque Baconao

Carisol-Los Corales $$$ *Carretera Baconao, km 54, Playa Cazonal; Tel. (22) 356113; fax (22) 356116.* A German-managed hotel in a picturesque setting at the eastern end of the biosphere park. Bungalows and mini-villas spaciously arranged among gardens. Good pool, scruffy beach. Mountain or sea views. 310 rooms.

Baracoa

Hotel El Castillo $$ *Calixto García, Loma del Paraíso; Tel. (21) 45164, fax (21) 45223.* One of Cuba's most charming hotels, converted from one of Baracoa's old forts. Perched on a cliff, it has a wonderful pool, gardens, magical views of El Yunque mountain, helpful staff, and spacious bedrooms. It is a real bargain. 35 rooms.

Hotel La Rusa $ *Máximo Gómez, no.161; Tel. (21) 42102.* Legendary little hotel that once belonged to Russian émigrée (La Rusa), renovated in 1990s. Che and Fidel both stayed here. Simple but not without charm. 12 rooms.

CASAS PARTICULARES (PRIVATE ACCOMMODATIONS)

Havana

Margarita Aguero $ *Calle Tejadillo, 52; Tel. (7) 673694.* A great value establishment: nice large room and separate bath, high ceilings, and use of large living room, all just minutes from the Plaza de la Catedral in Old Havana.

Casa Ines $ *Calle Segunda, no. 559 e/Ayestarán y Ayuntamiento, Plaza de la Revolución; Tel. (7) 870-0237.* Two comfortable rooms in a well-maintained, airy house in a good and safe location. Very friendly hosts.

Trinidad

Hostal Beltran I $ *on the hill near Church of Santa Ana.* Three comfortable rooms, all with private bath (two with balcony).

Casa Colonial Múñoz $ *José Martí, 401; Tel/fax (419) 3673.* Colonial house built in 1800; large rooms furnished with antiques, shady patio, and roof terrace. Knowledgeable young hosts. One of the finest *casas* in Cuba.

Casa Tica $ *Simón Bolívar, 459.* Comfortable colonial house with two rooms, ideally located on beautiful Plaza Mayor. Host Tica makes *santería* dolls. Great breakfasts.

Camagüey

Casa Manolo $ *Santa Rita, 8; Tel. (32) 294403.* Three comfortable rooms in large, cheery house in center of town. Friendly hosts. Also has a nice two-bedroom apartment.

Santiago de Cuba

Casa Magda $ *Bayamo, 31; Tel. (22) 624927.* One private, large room with bath in quiet house with sweet elderly woman. A five-minute walk from Plaza Céspedes. Good breakfasts.

Casa Hugo-Adela $ *San Basilio, 501; Tel. (22) 626359.* Rambling old house with apartment (kitchenette, private bath, separate entrance) on huge top terrace; spectacular views of city.

Recommended Restaurants

Dining choices in Cuba are hotels, state-owned restaurants, and *paladares* (private restaurants in people's homes). State restaurants can be overstaffed, the service slow, and the menu unreliable. As a general rule, the food served in hotels is better quality than in restaurants, but paladares can be best of all. *Paladares* had long existed clandestinely, but in 1994 the Cuban government legally permitted them (they pay hefty taxes and may have only 12 place settings). Many continue to circumvent the law and serve items on which the state maintains a monopoly: lobster, beef, and shrimp.

Arrive at restaurants by 8pm or earlier, as certain offerings might be sold out later. Reservations are almost never necessary except at the very busiest times of year.

The price categories below indicate the per-person cost for a three-course meal in US dollars, excluding drinks, tips, and shellfish (the latter is always far and away the costliest dish on the menu). Only restaurants in top hotels take credit cards, and American credit cards are not accepted (see page 118). For foreigners, it is very difficult to pay for meals in pesos.

$$$	over $25
$$	$12–$25
$	under $12

Old Havana

La Bodeguita del Medio $$ *Empredado, 207 e/ San Ignacio y Cuba; Tel. (7) 867-1374.* Open daily for lunch and dinner until late. Now in its seventh decade, this scruffy, graffiti-scrawled den has played host to celebrities from Sinatra to Salvador Allende to Hemingway. Now a constant stream of tourists sips *mojitos* along with good Creole cuisine.

La Divina Pastora $$–$$$ *Fortaleza de la Cabaña; Tel. (7) 860-8341.* Open daily for lunch and dinner. Take the tunnel under

the harbor to reach this stylish restaurant, set in a beautifully converted old battery by the waterside below the fort. Great view of
Havana skyline. Fish and seafood dishes and correct, swift service.

El Patio $$ *Plaza de la Catedral; Tel. (7) 867-1034.* Open 24
hours. One of the capital's romantic settings for a meal, in arguably
Havana's most splendidly painted and restored colonial courtyard.
Creole fare is decent, but it can't match the surroundings. The pop-
ular drinks terrace looks out on the Plaza de la Catedral.

La Paella $$ (Hostal Valencia) *Officios, 53 esq. Obrapía; Tel. (7)
867-1037.* Open daily for lunch and dinner (until late). The city's best
Spanish food—featuring rice dishes like paella, naturally—is found
at this charming inn. Comfortable and friendly; a good value.

Paladar Doña Eutimia $ *Callejón del Chorro (Plaza de la
Catedral).* Open daily for lunch and dinner. A cute little *paladar* just
off the cathedral square, in the front rooms of an old colonial house.
Portions of Spanish-Creole fare are large.

Paladar Sobrino $–$$ *Calle Obrapía, 458 e/ Aguacate y Villega.*
Open daily for lunch and dinner. A very professional *paladar* with
an extensive menu, tasty food, and ice-cold air conditioning.

Café Taberna Benny Moré $ *Mercaderes esq. a Teniente Rey (cor-
ner of Plaza Vieja); Tel. (7) 861-1637.* Open daily for lunch and dinner. In what was Havana's oldest café, Benny has been newly renovated in the exact style of the original and has good food at
surprisingly low prices. Live bands day and night; livelier at lunch.
A rare state-run restaurant offering good value and service.

Café del Oriente $$$ *Plaza de San Francisco; Tel. (7) 860-6686.*
Open daily for lunch and dinner (bar-café open 24 hours). This slick

international restaurant in a beautiful colonial mansion is where to go for that dress-up, blow-out meal. Extensive wine list.

Central Habana and New Havana

La Guarida $$ *Calle Concordia, 418, Centro Habana; Tel. (7) 862-4940.* Open daily for lunch and dinner. The most famous *paladar* in Havana, this atmospheric place (which has served the likes of Jack Nicholson, Pedro Almodóvar, and Queen Sofía of Spain) was where much of the Cuban film *Fresa y Chocolate* was filmed. Housed on the third floor of a great (and nearly gutted) Centro Habana house, it costs more than other *paladares* but is worth it for the ambience alone. Creative, wonderfully prepared food.

El Aljibe $$ *Av. 7 e/ 24 y 26, Miramar; Tel. (7) 204-1583.* Open daily for lunch and dinner. One of the best dining experiences in the capital is at this handsome, thatched-roof restaurant out in Miramar, offering top-flight Creole cooking. The specialty is the all-you-can-eat lemony chicken *(pollo asado El Ajibe),* with salad, plantains, french fries, rice, and beans. Popular with international businesspeople and diplomats, plus their Cuban dates.

Cojímar

La Terraza $$ *Calle Real y Candelaria; Tel. (7) 559232.* Founded in 1925, this charming waterside fish restaurant was once Hemingway's favorite and is now covered with evocative photos of the writer. Grilled fish and paella; nice bar.

Viñales

Ranchón San Vicente $$ *Carretera a Puerto Esperanza Km. 38, Pinar del Río; Tel. (82) 93200.* A rustically built country restaurant, surrounded by a farm dedicated to the breeding of game cocks. Open until 4pm. Try the broiled pork for lunch.

Casa de Don Tomás $–$$ *Valle de Viñales, Pinar del Río; Tel. (82) 93114.* Open for lunch and dinner. In a handsome colonial building dating from 1822. Good *criollo* specials.

Varadero

El Aljibe $–$$ *Av. 1ra. Calle 36; Tel. (45) 614019.* Open daily for lunch and dinner. The sister restaurant of one of Havana's best dining options (see above).

Las Américas $$$ *Av. Las Américas, Mansión Dupont (Xanadu); Tel. (45) 337013.* Open daily for dinner. Grand seaside mansion serving adventurous international dishes with variable success. Lunchtime snacks available on the terrace.

Mesón del Quijote $$–$$$ *Carretera Las Américas (Villa Cuba); Tel. (45) 667796.* Open daily for lunch and dinner. Toward the eastern end of the resort, serving quasi-Spanish cuisine in a pretty, candlelit dining room, with live music.

Mi Casita $$ *Camino del Mar e Calles 11 y 12; Tel. (45) 613787.* Open daily for dinner. Set meals in a nicely outfitted dining room on the beach. Very popular.

Cienfuegos

Palacio de Valle $$ *Calle 37 esq. 2, Punta Gorda; Tel. (432) 553201.* Open daily for lunch and dinner. Next to the Hotel Jagua, this ornate 19th-century Moorish palace (see page 58) has a ground-floor restaurant serving reasonable seafood and paella. Rooftop bar.

Trinidad

Sol y Son $ *Calle Simón Bolívar, 283.* Open daily for lunch and dinner. A colonial house with an entryway that might be an antiques

Cuba

shop and peaceful courtyard, offering such tasty dishes as *cerdo borracho* (drunk pork, with rum) and stuffed fish.

El Jigüe $–$$ *Rubén M. Villena esq. P. Guinart; Tel. (419) 4315.* Open daily for lunch and only occasionally for dinner. An attractive, airy colonial house with a gloriously painted façade and terrace leading onto one of Trinidad's prettiest squares. Wide range of international and Cuban dishes, nicely done.

Santa Ana $$ *Santo Domingo (Plaza de Santa Ana); Tel. (419) 3523.* Open daily for lunch and dinner. A former prison on the old town's edge, handsomely restored to include a stylish restaurant off its glowing orange courtyard and a cool bar overlooking the dilapidated Santa Ana church. Popular with tour groups on day trips.

Camagüey

Campana de Toledo $ *Plaza de San Juan de Dios; Tel. (32) 295888.* Open daily for lunch. Good—if not memorable—Spanish and Creole fare in one of the city's prettiest courtyards. Live music.

Guardalavaca

El Ancla $$ *Playa Guardalavaca, Banes; Tel. (24) 30237.* Open daily for lunch and dinner. Seafood platters and pastas and a waterside cocktail terrace in a fabulous site at the eastern end of the beach (cross the beach and river to reach it).

Santiago de Cuba

Doña Nelly $–$$ *Avenida Carnicería, 412 e/ San Francisco y San Gerónimo; Tel. (22) 652195.* Open daily for breakfast, lunch, and dinner. A cozy little *paladar* just off of the main commercial thoroughfare, Enramada. Excellent chicken and pork dishes (like *chuleta de cerdo*) in large portions; air conditioning.

Gilda's Paladar $–$$ *Calle San Basilio, 116 e/ Padre Piro y Tte. Rey.* Open daily for lunch and dinner. One of the city's best-known *paladares,* to which groups of kid hustlers will try to take you. Go on your own for the comfortable, exposed-brick (and graffiti-covered) dining room and good dishes from spaghetti to lobster. Operated by a group of young women.

El Morro $$ *Carretera del Morro; Tel. (22) 687151.* Open daily for lunch and dinner. In a superb clifftop location on a vine-covered terrace next to El Morro castle, this restaurant might be the best in Santiago, offering excellent Creole fare along with the coastal views.

Santiago 1900 $–$$ *Bartolomé Masó, 354, e/ Hartmann y Pío Rosado; Tel. (22) 623507.* Open daily for lunch and dinner. This spectacular mansion, which once belonged to the Bacardí rum family, has a beautiful courtyard and two terraces upstairs. You can pay in pesos, which makes a meal absurdly cheap (but there may be only one main course available). The *criollo* cooking is mostly hit or miss, as are the *mojitos;* try fried chicken or *carne asado* (roasted meats).

Tocororo $$$ *Avenida Manduley, 57, esq. 7, Vista Alegre; Tel. (22) 641369.* Open daily for lunch and dinner. As close as Cuba gets to nouvelle cuisine, with an expensive lobster and fish. The setting is a posh villa.

Baracoa

La Colonial $ *José Martí, 123; Tel. (21) 43161.* Open daily for lunch and dinner. Of Baracoa's many good *paladares,* this is one of the nicest, with a seductive ambience and such local fare as coconut-flavored fish-and-rice dishes and sweet *cucurucho.*

INDEX

143